VEGAN for everyone

FAMILY FRIENDLY RECIPES WITH A DELICIOUS, MODERN TWIST

LAURA THEODORE

THE BEST OF JAZZY VEGETARIAN

Scribe Publishing Company
Royal Oak, Michigan

Scribe Publishing Company
29488 Woodward, Suite 426
Royal Oak, MI 48073
www.scribe-publishing.com

Vegan for Everyone: 160 Family Friendly Recipes with a Delicious, Modern Twist

Interior food photos: Laura Theodore, Andy Ebberbach, David Kaplan, Joe Orecchio, Robert White, Julie Snyder and Jacob Fisher
Additional photos: Annie Oliverio, pages 46, 47, 54, 113, 158, 201, 246 and 281
Additional photos: Warren Jefferson, pages 67, 128, 151, 179, 203 and 209
Front cover photo: Joe Orecchio
Back cover photos by: Andy Ebberbach, Annie Oliverio and Laura Theodore

Editors: Jennifer Baum, Mel Corrigan and Kit Emory
Copy editing by: William Lacy and Allison Janicki
Cover and interior design: John Wincek, Aerocraft Charter Art Service

Hair and makeup for cover photo: Victoria De Los Rios
Laura's makeup provided in part by: Graftobian Make-Up Company
Dinnerware provided in part by: Cardinal International
Table linens provided in part by: April Cornell
Fresh produce provided in part by: Melissa's Produce

PRINTED IN THE UNITED STATES OF AMERICA

ISBN: 978-0-9916021-6-2

Publisher's Cataloging-in-Publication data

Names: Theodore, Laura, author.
Title: Vegan for everyone : 160 family friendly recipes with a delicious , modern twist / Laura Theodore.
Description: Includes index. | Royal Oak, MI: Scribe Publishing Company, 2020.
Identifiers: LCCN 2019947874 | ISBN 978-0-9916021-6-2
Subjects: LCSH Vegan cooking—United States. | Veganism. | Cooking, American. | Cookbooks. | BISAC COOKING / Vegan
Classification: LCC TX837 .T4555 2020 | DDC 641.5636—dc23

Today is the day to start living more compassionately.

LAURA THEODORE

To all of the animals—this book is for you.

"Laura Theodore's *Vegan for Everyone* is a comprehensive cookbook that puts a vegan splash on your favorite recipes! From classic breakfast fare to the ultimate chocolate desserts, Laura has you covered. Don't miss her guides to filling your spice rack with exciting flavors or stocking your pantry with the essential ingredients. You won't want to put this cookbook down!"

Neal Barnard, MD, FACC, president, Physicians Committee for Responsible Medicine

"I adore Laura's books! *Vegan for Everyone* has the yummiest recipes! You will love these easy recipes that include sandwiches, pastas, pizzas and mouthwatering desserts. There is even a 'Chocolate Only' chapter! Oh my!"

Chloe Coscarelli, vegan chef and cookbook author

"*Vegan for Everyone* truly is for everyone! Laura has veganized favorite classic recipes using ingredients that are easy to find in just about any grocery store. These mouthwatering recipes cover everything from everyday meals and snacks to dinner party fare and holiday menus. These meals are deliciously fun and they come together quickly. You'll find yourself excited to get into the kitchen so you can cook your way through this book!"

Dianne Wenz, author, *The Truly Healthy Vegan Cookbook*

"Laura Theodore's new cookbook, *Vegan for Everyone*, is as jazzy as she is. You can make restaurant quality food your whole family will love. Laura is as talented on camera as she is at cooking; you can rest assured that her recipes will get you from hungry to satisfied. Her new cookbook is a great addition to any kitchen."

Christa Clark, ArtisticVegan.com

"Laura Theodore's *Vegan for Everyone* really is for everyone. These recipes are not just for people eating a plant-based diet; these recipes are for anyone who loves delicious, fabulous food. I'm inspired to start cooking again!"

Pamela A. Popper, PhD, ND, president, Wellness Forum Health

"The ever-innovative Jazzy Vegetarian returns with this stunning cookbook that offers truly kitchen-friendly recipes so easy that everyone will find them compelling. All the classic dishes you've loved and enjoyed through the years are included in this beautiful volume, complete with lip-smacking, irresistibly gorgeous photos that seem to reach out and guide you to the dining table. This book will be treasured in every kitchen."

Zel and Reuben Allen, Vegetarians in Paradise

"This vegan cookbook from Laura Theodore, a master at plant-based cooking, is *the* essential cookbook you need on your shelf—you will turn to it time and time again to make easy plant-based meals every day."

Sharon Palmer, MSFS, RDN, The Plant-Powered Dietitian

"Laura Theodore takes such great joy in creating fabulously festive fare (that's also easy enough to enjoy every day) that it's almost easy to forget—but let's not!—that she's driven by her compassion for animals and concern for the planet. I'm so excited to have this "best of" collection, featuring fan favorites from her multi-season *Jazzy Vegetarian* series, as well as her own favorites. And what a rich selection it is—from breakfast and baking to one-pot meals and divine desserts, and so much more in between. Whether this is your first vegan cookbook or you have shelves filled with them, I assure you that this is one that you'll actually use, all year round."

Nava Atlas, author of *5-Ingredient Vegan* and many others

"For a decade, Laura has shared her passion for plant-based eating in her *Jazzy Vegetarian* show. Now she's placed fan-based favorites and 'best of' recipes inside these pages. Whether she's keeping it simple with the basics, whipping up comfort foods or sharing new creations, these recipes are easy and stress-free to prepare and simply delicious."

Ann Gentry, author, *The Real Food Daily Cookbook* and *Real Food for Everyone*

Table of Contents

Jazzy Vegetarian gratefully thanks and

acknowledges our Season Eight sponsors,

EARTH FARE and **PAPA VINCE,**

whose generous support has made it possible

to share these recipes with the world.

HEALTHY FOOD FOR EVERYONE

Jazzy Vegetarian gratefully acknowledges our past sponsors:

Soom®

Tropicana

It's been almost ten years since *Jazzy Vegetarian* premiered on public television across the nation, and we are celebrating this remarkable milestone with a "best of" book.

CHAPTER

ONE

Introduction

From weekday family fare to holiday soirée menus and every other meal in between, I have compiled the "cream of the vegan crop" dishes from *all* of my cookbooks, including fan favorites from each season of the television series, many of my personal favorite recipes and over one hundred *new* delicious *and* nutritious recipes to make planning, preparing and serving plant-based meals easier for you, while being kinder to animals and our planet.

This diverse vegan recipe collection highlights quick-to-prepare entrées, festive dishes, three-ingredient recipes, satisfying sides, one-pot meals, breakfast and lunch classics and rich-tasting desserts, along with an entire chapter of pasta "impostors," a wide array of vegan burgers and an entire section devoted to decadent chocolate vegan treats.

New for this book, I have included plenty of gluten-free recipes, designated with a convenient icon to let you know if the recipe is gluten free or has a gluten-free option. The recipes in this cookbook are family friendly and all include in-depth instructions, incorporating ingredients that are easy to find in most major supermarkets.

I would like to take this opportunity to thank everyone who has supported our journey, tuned in each week, written us awesome, complimentary emails and those who have loved our show from day one! I am so grateful, too, that we continue to connect with so many new viewers each season, with the series now being available in over ninety percent of U.S. households! We could not have done it without you!

My goal is that this volume of well-loved recipes will make your life easier, healthier and ultimately happier with yummy meal choices and tasty fare designed to please every person you are cooking for. This book truly is: *Vegan for Everyone!* Now let's get started.

I find certain ingredients to be essential in my daily cooking. Here's my short list of basic items, along with brief information about of some of the unusual or fundamental ingredients featured in this book. I hope this chapter makes your kitchen endeavors easier, more efficient and more enjoyable.

CHAPTER

TWO

Best Vegan Essentials

ABOUT THE RECIPES

GLUTEN-FREE OPTION

All of the recipes in this book are vegan: they do not use any dairy, eggs, meat or any other animal ingredients, including honey.

Many of the recipes in this book are gluten free, too. Throughout the book, an icon signifies recipes that are gluten free. Many additional recipes include alternate instructions for gluten-free preparation, and these recipes will have a gluten-free option icon.

Many foods like tofu, tomato or marinara sauce, miso, tahini, tempeh, tamari, ketchup, mustard, vegan cheese and many other common ingredients can sometimes contain gluten. If you must follow a gluten-free diet for health reasons, be sure to purchase certified gluten-free ingredients and consult with a medical professional on the best dietary guidelines for you. In addition, if you are adopting a vegan diet, please consult a registered dietitian or your practitioner regarding your needs for supplementation.

Quick Meal Options

For those really busy days, we have highlighted the three-ingredient recipes throughout the book with an icon, too!

I hope these added features make your meal preparation a little easier and a lot more fun!

ESSENTIAL INGREDIENTS

Here's my list of basic or specialized ingredients used within the pages of this book, including information about each item. Most of these foods can be purchased from major supermarkets or health food stores, but most can be easily ordered online, too.

Brown rice (short grain, long grain): Brown rice is rice that has not been hulled, leaving the outer layer of bran on the grain, making it more nutrient-dense than refined white rice. Brown rice has a slightly nutty flavor and is chewier than refined white rice. Dry brown rice *can* become rancid when stored at room temperature, so refrigerate it after opening.

Brown sugar, cane sugar and raw cane turbinado sugar, vegan: Dark brown sugar has a distinctive molasses taste that gives recipes a sweet, rich flavor. Cane sugar is my "go-to" sweetener when baking cakes or cookies that need to be lighter in both texture and color. Some sugars are filtered and bleached with bone char, which is why many refined white sugars are unsuitable for vegans. Several vegan-friendly sugar companies can be found online, and vegan sugar can be purchased at most major supermarkets.

Canned beans (black, kidney, white, pinto and garbanzo): Canned beans make a great base for creating quick, hearty, nutrient-dense, protein- *and* fiber-rich vegan meals. Beans are inexpensive and extremely versatile. I use canned beans for creating dips, vegan burgers, burritos, soups, casseroles, salads, appetizers and so much more. Canned beans are great for supplying convenience to your weekly menu plan. Look to purchase organic beans packed in cans made with BPA-free lining. Refrigerate canned beans after opening.

Cheese, vegan: This "cheese" is easily substituted for dairy cheese in most recipes, and a wide variety of flavors are available in supermarkets and health food stores. Look for the "V" on the label to ensure it is dairy free and animal free. If you follow a gluten-free diet, purchase certified gluten-free vegan cheese, now available in many supermarkets. Whenever you see the word *cheeze* in this cookbook, it denotes a recipe that includes homemade vegan "cheese."

Cocoa powder, unsweetened: Cocoa powder is made by grinding cacao beans and pressing out the cocoa butter, resulting in a dense powder that's low in fat but high in flavor. It adds a rich chocolate taste to baked goods and puddings. Try buying organic, fair-trade, non-alkalized cocoa powder whenever it is available, and read the label to be sure it's dairy free (and gluten free, if needed!).

Dark chocolate, vegan: Good quality dark chocolate is made by adding sugar and fat (typically cocoa butter) to ground cacao beans, the seeds from cacao (chocolate) trees. For the best vegan choice, purchase chocolate that is fair trade, organic and dairy free. For a deeper, rich taste, purchase dark chocolate that is labeled as containing at least fifty-five percent or higher cacao content. For a gluten-free option, purchase chocolate that is certified gluten free.

Extra-virgin olive oil: This rich and flavorful fruit oil is simply the juice pressed from olives. It is delicious in salad dressings, casseroles, soups, sauces, stews or as a dip for crusty bread. You might also lightly sauté vegetables in olive oil or use it as a substitute for butter in baked goods. Store olive oil in a dark, cool place.

Flaxseeds (golden or brown): Flaxseeds have an impressive omega-3 fatty acid content and are high in both soluble and insoluble fiber. Before using flaxseeds, make certain to grind them with a high-performance blending appliance (or a grain mill or coffee grinder designated for flaxseeds only). The nutritional value of flaxseeds is released when they are ground. To replace one egg in many baked goods recipes, mix 1 tablespoon freshly ground flaxseeds with 3 tablespoons water.

Maple syrup: Maple syrup is made from sap extracted from various types of maple trees. Purchase pure, organic maple syrup to avoid undesirable additives. Recently, the grading system for maple syrup was changed. All *100% pure maple syrup* is now classified as "Grade A." ("Grade B" maple syrup labeling no longer exists.)

Here's a basic overview of the new "Grade A" maple syrup classifications:

GOLDEN COLOR, DELICATE TASTE: This is the lightest of the maple syrup grades, best for drizzling over waffles, pancakes or ice cream.

AMBER COLOR, RICH TASTE: This grade of maple syrup is a little more flavorful and works well when cooking and baking.

DARK COLOR, ROBUST TASTE: This grade of maple syrup is high in flavor and is used for recipes that require a full-bodied maple taste. I like to use this grade of maple syrup in many of my recipes.

VERY DARK COLOR, STRONG TASTE: This grade of maple syrup is very strong tasting and may be best used as a substitute for molasses.

Buttery spread or margarine, vegan: Vegan buttery spread, vegan "margarine" and vegan butter are sold in tubs or sticks. Buy a vegan "butter" that is non-GMO (free of genetically modified ingredients), organic and free of hydrogenated oils. Spread it on baked goods or use it in any recipe that calls for butter or margarine.

Marinara sauce and canned tomatoes, vegan: A good, jarred vegan marinara sauce makes a time-saving staple for recipes such as lasagna, chili, sauces, casseroles, stews and more. Keep several jars stocked in your pantry for use when time is at a premium. Canned tomatoes provide the same flexibility for creating easy meals. I keep organic diced, crushed and fire-roasted canned (BPA-free) tomato varieties on hand. Be sure to refrigerate marinara sauce and/or canned tomatoes after opening. Note that not all brands of vegan marinara sauce (*or* canned tomatoes) are gluten free, so purchase certified gluten-free sauce if you *are* on a gluten-free diet.

Mayonnaise, vegan: Egg-free vegan mayonnaise can be used in place of traditional mayonnaise in most recipes. It is often soy-, safflower- or grapeseed-based. Found in health food stores and most supermarkets, vegan mayonnaise is usually displayed in the refrigerated section or sometimes found in the condiment aisle. Vegan mayonnaise is perfect to use in pasta or potato salad or as a base for homemade dips and salad dressings. You can use *Very Delicious Vegan Mayonnaise* (page 83) in any recipe that calls for vegan mayonnaise in this book.

Medjool dates: The Medjool date is the fruit of the date palm tree. There are many varieties of dates, but Medjool dates are generally larger and sweeter, so they are ideal to use in baked goods, smoothies, raw pie crusts and many desserts. On their own, they make a great snack. Yum!

Miso: A culinary staple in Japan, miso is a thick, salty, fermented paste made with soybeans, sometimes in combination with other beans, grains or additional ingredients. It can be used to enhance the flavor of dips, sauces, soups, spreads, stews and more. I typically use mellow white miso, which has a delicate flavor; however, any variety of light miso is fine for the recipes in this book. When adding miso to hot foods, stir it into the food just before serving, as high heat destroys its beneficial enzymes. To help distribute miso evenly in hot foods, mix it into a bit of warm water or broth before adding it to the dish. If you are following a gluten-free diet, be sure to purchase certified gluten-free miso.

Nondairy milk: Nondairy milk, once relegated to the shelves of natural foods stores, is now available in mainstream supermarkets. You'll find a number of varieties beyond soymilk, made with almonds, coconut, cashews, oats, rice, hempseeds, flaxseeds or rice. It comes in unsweetened, plain and flavored versions. Choose unsweetened, plain nondairy milk for savory recipes. The flavored and/or sweetened varieties are ideal for smoothies, baking, pouring over cereal or just plain sipping.

Nori (toasted seaweed sheets): Nori is one of the tastiest sea vegetables. Good quality nori has a sweet, delicate flavor and is a good source of minerals, vitamins, iodine and protein. Use toasted nori sheets for making sushi or nori rolls, or grind them in a blender and sprinkle the powder in salads or soups.

Nuts and seeds: In addition to being an excellent source of protein, nuts and seeds have vitamins, minerals, fiber, essential amino acids *and* healthy fats! I love to use nuts and seeds for preparing plant-based burgers, meatless loaves, nut "cheezes," vegan creams and salad dressings. They add crunch and nutrition to salads and steamed vegetables. I use almonds, pecans, walnuts, cashews, sunflower seeds, flaxseeds (see page 10 for a detailed description of flaxseeds) and more. Be sure to refrigerate nuts and seeds after opening.

Quinoa: This excellent alternative to brown rice is technically a seed, not a grain, but its texture, taste and preparation method echo that of many whole grains, so it is often categorized as a grain. Uncooked quinoa requires thorough rinsing before cooking. Quinoa is a nutritional powerhouse, high in quality protein and delightful when used as a stuffing for sweet bell peppers, mushrooms or squash, and it's delicious served alongside a plate of steamed vegetables. I sometimes cook quinoa with canned beans to make a quick and hearty supper. Chilled, cooked quinoa makes a great base for a cold summer salad or reheated and served with nondairy milk to make a hearty breakfast porridge. Quinoa also makes an excellent thickener and protein-booster for stews, soups and casseroles.

JAZZY TIP: *When I travel I combine nuts and seeds—like walnuts, sunflower seeds, pecans, cashews, brazil nuts and almonds—and pack them into a re-sealable bag for a quick "pick me up" throughout my trip.*

Rolled Oats (organic, quick cooking and old fashioned, gluten-free): Rolled oats are made from the whole grains of oats that are sometimes steamed (to make them soft and pliable) and then pressed to flatten them. Rolled oats cook faster than steel-cut oats, and besides the traditional morning bowl of hearty oatmeal, I like to use rolled oats in cookies, muffins, pie crusts, crisps, quick breads, meatless loaves and vegan burgers. Quick cooking rolled oats are simply oats that are rolled and cut thinner than old fashioned rolled oats to shorten the cooking time. To make homemade oat flour, pour some rolled oats into a blender and process into coarse or fine flour. If you are cooking gluten free, be certain to buy certified gluten-free rolled oats. If you do not have the need to cook gluten free, you may use regular rolled oats (quick cooking or old fashioned) in any of the recipes in this book that call for gluten-free oats.

Salsa: There are many varieties of jarred salsa available in most supermarkets. Keep jars of salsa stocked in your pantry as they can be used to enhance recipes such as chili, soups, guacamole and casseroles. Salsa is also great served alongside dippers, such as whole-grain tortilla chips or veggie sticks.

Seitan: Made from wheat, seitan is otherwise known as "wheat meat." It is high in protein and becomes similar to meat in appearance, flavor and texture when cooked. I like using seitan in hearty dishes like lasagna, casseroles, shish kebabs and veggie sautés. Prepared seitan can be found in the refrigerated section of most health food stores and well-stocked supermarkets, usually near the tofu.

Tahini: Tahini is made by grinding hulled (or unhulled) sesame seeds into a creamy paste. Tahini is traditionally used in hummus, but I use it in cookies, pie crusts, salad dressings, smoothies, vegan burgers, meatless loaves and more. Tahini is available in jars or cans and is found in health food stores or in the nut butter or ethnic food section of well-stocked supermarkets.

Tamari, gluten-free: Tamari sauce is rich and mellow-tasting, with a more complex flavor profile than ordinary soy sauce. Traditionally, tamari is made with whole, fermented soybeans with little or no wheat, giving it a richer and milder taste than regular soy sauce. (If you are cooking gluten free, be *sure* to buy certified gluten-free tamari.) I like to use organic tamari that is MSG-free, certified gluten free and made with non-GMO soybeans. Gluten-free reduced-sodium tamari can be used interchangeably in any recipe in this book that calls for tamari.

Reduced-sodium tamari has about 25 percent less sodium than regular tamari. Use tamari as a flavor booster in sauces, casseroles, pasta dishes and vegan gravy. It pairs beautifully with stir-fries, steamed vegetables, stews and soups to help create a smooth but full flavor. It also adds great taste to both sweet and savory marinades for tofu, tempeh, mushrooms or squash. Of note: gluten-free tamari is widely available, but if you are not restricting your gluten intake, you may use regular (non-GMO) tamari in any of the recipes in this book that call for gluten-free tamari. If you require a *soy-free* seasoning, you may substitute *gluten-free coconut aminos* for any recipe in this book that calls for gluten-free tamari.

Tempeh (non-GMO, organic): Tempeh is made from the controlled fermentation of soybeans. There are many tasty varieties available, such as five-grain or three-grain tempeh. Always buy non-GMO, organic tempeh from a reputable source. Tempeh is used in sandwiches, casseroles, stews and soups. Try tempeh lightly steamed and served on top of steamed veggies or a crisp green salad. Once you get the hang of cooking with tempeh, you'll want to make it a staple in your diet. If you are following a gluten-free diet, be sure to purchase certified gluten-free tempeh.

Tofu (non-GMO, organic): This versatile soy food has been a popular mainstay in vegetarian and vegan diets for decades. Tofu is made from soybeans, water and a coagulant. It is widely available in supermarkets. Plain tofu comes in two main forms: regular (packed in water and refrigerated) and silken (in aseptic cartons and refrigerated tubs). Each type is available in soft, firm and extra-firm varieties. Tofu is superb in casseroles, stir-fries, soups, puddings, smoothies and as a ricotta cheese substitute in dishes like lasagna or vegetable casseroles. Baked tofu can be purchased in various flavors, such as smoked, Italian-style, lemon pepper and several Asian-flavored varieties. Purchase certified gluten-free tofu if you are on a gluten-restricted diet. There are several varieties of gluten-free tofu available in most supermarkets.

Vegetable broth and bouillon cubes: Keep several aseptic cartons of organic vegetable broth in your pantry to enhance soups, stews, chili, sauces, vegan gravies and casseroles. Vegetable bouillon cubes are handy to use in the same way. Purchase organic vegan cubes and make sure they are free of hydrogenated oils. If you are gluten free, choose a gluten-free brand.

Wheat germ: Wheat germ, the embryo of the wheat kernel, is dense in flavor, texture and nutrients, especially protein, some B vitamins and healthful fats. It should be refrigerated after opening to prevent it from becoming rancid. Wheat germ is available in supermarkets and natural food stores in both raw and toasted forms. Toasted wheat germ has a deliciously nutty flavor and a pleasant, crunchy texture. Sprinkle it over pasta instead of parmesan cheese or over a casserole instead of bread crumbs. Toasted wheat germ can also be used to enhance the flavor and texture of baked goods.

Whole-grain flour, bread and tortillas (vegan and/or gluten-free): Flours, breads and pasta made with one hundred percent whole grains are considered to have a superior nutritional profile to refined grains, offering a complex, full-bodied texture and flavor to your recipes. Look for the word "whole" on the package label and buy certified organic flour, bread and tortillas whenever available. If you are looking for vegan bread, read the label to make certain there are no animal products like honey, eggs or milk hidden in the ingredients. I like to buy whole-grain, seeded bread for extra nutritional value. When seeking gluten-free *and* vegan bread (or tortillas) in your supermarket, look in the freezer case where other frozen natural foods are stocked. Check the labels carefully to make certain the product is both gluten free *and* vegan!

ESSENTIAL FOR YOUR SPICE RACK

Cooking with dried herbs and spices is an easy way to add layers of flavor to your dishes. I regularly incorporate dried herbs and spices into my recipes. One of my favorite ways to save time in the kitchen is to use pre-mixed seasonings, such as all-purpose seasoning or *Italian seasoning blend* (recipe page 96). For example, when I want to give my recipes an Italian accent, I grab just *one jar* of Italian seasoning blend and I use that instead of *six or seven jars* of herbs (like basil, oregano, thyme, sage, rosemary and marjoram). Pre-mixed herb and spice blends really make it a lot easier and less time-consuming to get a mouthwatering meal on the table!

Here's my go-to list of dried herbs, spices and seasoning blends that I like to keep stocked on my spice rack.

All-Purpose Seasoning Blend
Basil
Black Pepper, in grinder
Cayenne Pepper
Chili Powder
Cinnamon (Ceylon), ground
Cumin
Dill Weed
Garam Masala
Garlic Powder
Italian Seasoning Blend
Marjoram
Oregano
Paprika, regular and smoked
Parsley
Pumpkin Pie Spice
Red Pepper Flakes, crushed
Rosemary, crushed
Sea salt and/or Himalayan Pink Salt
Turmeric, ground

Salt and Pepper—"Yes, Please!" or "No, Thanks!"?

Why aren't exact amounts of salt and pepper included in some of the recipes in this book? If a recipe requires a precise amount of salt or pepper to make it taste optimal, the exact amount is included in the ingredients list. If the inclusion of either salt or pepper is only a matter of choice, I have left it up to you to season as desired.

TABLE OF EQUIVALENT MEASURES

No matter how many times I measure ingredients in my recipes, I never seem to remember the table of equivalent measures. This table is convenient to refer to when doubling or tripling recipes, cooking up new recipes or cutting an existing recipe in half. I know you'll find this list as handy as I do!

THIS...	EQUALS THIS...
3 teaspoons	1 tablespoon
4 tablespoons	¼ cup
5 tablespoons plus 1 teaspoon	⅓ cup
8 tablespoons	½ cup
12 tablespoons	¾ cup
16 tablespoons	1 cup (or 8 ounces)
2 cups	1 pint (or 16 ounces)
4 cups	1 quart (or 32 ounces)
4 quarts	1 gallon (or 128 ounces)

Now, let's get to the recipes! Wishing you happy, healthy cooking!

Breakfast does just that—it *breaks* our overnight *fast*. Smoothies make a great option for breakfast on the go, while dishes like scrambled tofu, a grain-based casserole, oatmeal and fruit crumble, vegan quiche or gluten-free pancakes provide hearty choices to satisfy robust appetites. Whatever your breakfast style, you'll find some *jazzylicious* recipes in this chapter to start your day the right way!

CHAPTER

THREE

Breakfast Classics

No-Egg Tofu-Veggie Scramble, *page 34*

GLUTEN-FREE

This frosty-licious smoothie makes an invigorating breakfast treat! The refreshing taste of the orange complements the fresh blueberries, and the frozen bananas add a refreshing, creamy texture. Yum.

Frosty BLUEBERRY-ORANGE SMOOTHIE

MAKES 1 TO 2 SERVINGS

1 cup fresh blueberries

1 medium orange, peeled, seeded and chopped

1 large peeled, sliced and frozen banana

½ to ¾ cup nondairy milk, your preferred variety, plus more as needed

3 to 4 ice cubes (optional, see note)

CHEF'S NOTE: *You may use frozen blueberries and omit the ice cubes, if desired.*

Put all of the ingredients in a high-performance blending appliance and process until smooth and creamy, adding more nondairy milk as needed to create the desired consistency.

Easy to whip up first thing in the morning, this comforting favorite will please adults and kiddos alike!

YUMMY BANANA-OAT *Pancakes*

MAKES 8 TO 10 PANCAKES

- 1 cup gluten-free, quick cooking rolled oats
- ¾ cup plus 3 tablespoons unsweetened nondairy milk, plus more as needed (see note)
- 1 slightly rounded cup peeled and thinly sliced banana
- 1 teaspoon baking powder
- 1 tablespoon extra-virgin olive oil, plus more for griddle
- 2 tablespoons maple syrup, plus more for serving
- ¼ teaspoon sea salt
- Blueberries, for serving (optional, see variation)

Preheat the oven to 200 degrees F. Line a large, rimmed baking sheet with unbleached parchment paper.

To make the batter, put all of the ingredients in a blender and process until smooth. Put a small amount of olive oil in a large, nonstick griddle or skillet over medium heat. Heat the griddle until a drop of water skitters across the surface. *(Recipe continues on page 22.)*

CHEF'S NOTE: *For a sweeter pancake with a hint of vanilla flavor, use sweetened vanilla flavored nondairy milk in place of the unsweetened variety.*

VARIATIONS:

Chocolate Chip Pancakes

Add 5 to 6 vegan chocolate chips to each pancake right after the batter is poured into the pan.

Blueberry Pancakes

Add 5 to 6 small fresh blueberries to each pancake right after the batter is poured into the pan.

For each pancake, pour ¼ cup of batter onto the griddle. Depending on the size of your griddle (or skillet), you should be able to cook 3 to 6 pancakes in each batch. Cook for 2 to 3 minutes until the underside is golden and bubbles form on top. Flip each pancake and cook the other side for about 2 minutes, or until the underside of the pancake is golden brown. Repeat with the remaining batter until all pancakes are cooked. As the batter sits, it will thicken *very* quickly. Before cooking subsequent batches, you may need to stir in a *tiny* bit—2 teaspoons or so—more nondairy milk into the batter so that it is not too thick for pouring.

After each batch of pancakes cook, put them in a single layer on the lined baking sheet and keep them warm in the oven until serving. Serve with plenty of maple syrup topped with some fresh berries, if desired.

This delightful crumble is quick-to-prep, satisfying and truly delicious. It serves triple duty as a breakfast treat, healthful dessert or fruit-full afternoon snack!

APPLE, BANANA AND CRANBERRY *Crumble*

MAKES 4 TO 6 SERVINGS

APPLE LAYER

1 teaspoon extra-virgin olive oil (for coating casserole dish)

4 medium tart green and/or sweet red apples, cored and sliced (do not peel)

4 heaping tablespoons sweetened dried cranberries

3½ tablespoons maple syrup

1 rounded teaspoon ground cinnamon

OAT LAYER

1 very large ripe banana, peeled (see note)

1 tablespoon maple syrup, plus more for serving

1 rounded teaspoon ground cinnamon

1¼ cups gluten-free rolled oats (quick cooking *or* old fashioned)

Preheat the oven to 350 degrees F. Lightly coat a 9- x 12-inch or similarly sized casserole dish with 1 teaspoon olive oil.

To make the apple layer, put the apples in a medium-sized bowl. Add the cranberries, 3½ tablespoons maple syrup and 1 teaspoon ground cinnamon. Stir the mixture with a large spoon to combine. Transfer to the prepared casserole dish.

To make the oat layer, put the banana, 1 tablespoon maple syrup and 1 rounded teaspoon ground cinnamon into a medium-sized bowl. Mash together using a potato masher or large fork until almost smooth, allowing a few small chunks to remain. Add the rolled oats and mix with a large spoon to combine. Spread the banana/oat mixture over the apples in an even layer.

Cover and bake for 35 to 40 minutes or until the apples are soft. Uncover and bake for an additional 5 minutes, or until the topping is slightly crisp. Transfer the casserole to a wire rack, and let cool for 5 minutes before serving. Spoon into shallow bowls and serve with maple syrup on the side, if desired. Tightly covered and stored in the refrigerator, the crumble will keep for 1 day.

CHEF'S NOTE: *If you do not have a large banana, use 1½ medium ripe bananas or 2 small ripe bananas.*

GLUTEN-FREE

This hearty bowl makes for substantial breakfast fare. Baked in the oven, it's a great choice for busy mornings. This recipe can be easily doubled or tripled to feed a crowd!

Coconut-y RICE BREAKFAST CASSEROLE

MAKES 3 TO 4 SERVINGS

1 cup *uncooked* long grain brown rice

½ cup unsweetened shredded dried coconut

½ teaspoon ground cinnamon

½ teaspoon vanilla extract

6 large Medjool dates, pitted and chopped

3 cups water

2 tablespoons maple syrup, plus more for serving

Nondairy milk, for serving

Preheat the oven to 375 degrees F. Put the rice, coconut, cinnamon, vanilla and dates into a medium-sized casserole dish with a tight-fitting lid. Stir to combine. Pour the water over the rice mixture and gently stir to combine.

Cover and bake for 40 to 45 minutes, or until the water is almost absorbed and the rice is soft. Remove from the oven, uncover and drizzle 2 tablespoons maple syrup over the top. Cover and bake for 5 to 10 minutes more until all water is absorbed. Put the dish on a wire rack and let stand for 20 minutes before serving. Serve with nondairy milk and more maple syrup on the side, if desired.

GLUTEN-FREE

Cookies for breakfast? Yep, kids of all ages are gonna love 'em. These cookies are a great grab-n-go option when morning time is at a premium. Plus, they make a healthy afternoon snack or nutritious dessert. Wow.

OATMEAL-BANANA BREAKFAST *Cookies*

MAKES 12 TO 16 COOKIES

3 tablespoons golden flaxseeds

1¼ cups gluten-free, old fashioned rolled oats

1⅓ cups peeled and sliced bananas

⅓ cup maple syrup

1 rounded tablespoon sesame tahini (purchase certified gluten-free tahini if you are gluten-free)

½ teaspoon ground cinnamon

⅓ cup raisins

Preheat the oven to 400 degrees F. Line a large, rimmed baking sheet with unbleached parchment paper.

Put the flaxseeds in a high-performance blending appliance and process into fine flour. Put the flaxseed flour into a large bowl. Add the oats and stir to combine.

Put the sliced bananas, maple syrup, tahini and cinnamon in a medium-sized bowl. Using a potato masher, mash until almost smooth, leaving some chunky bits of banana. Add the banana mixture to the oat mixture and stir to combine. Fold in the raisins.

Drop a heaping tablespoonful of the cookie dough onto the prepared sheet and flatten slightly with a rubber spatula. Continue in this manner with the remaining dough. Bake for 15 to 20 minutes, or until the edges are golden brown and cookies are almost set. Transfer the cookies to a wire rack and cool for 8 to 10 minutes. Stored in an airtight container in the refrigerator, the cookies will keep for about 3 days.

Just like "moms" used to make, sans the eggs. I say "moms" because both my mother *and* my husband's mother made an egg-based version of this savory breakfast delicacy when we were young. If you try it once, you'll be hooked!

Rocky Mountain TOAST

MAKES 4 SERVINGS

1 block (14 to 16 ounces) **firm or extra-firm regular tofu, drained** (see note)

½ cup shredded vegan cheese (see note)

½ teaspoon ground turmeric

¼ teaspoon gluten-free tamari

⅛ teaspoon sea salt

Freshly ground black pepper, to taste

4 very large slices vegan whole-grain or gluten-free bread (see notes)

1 tablespoon vegan buttery spread, plus more as needed

CHEF'S NOTE: *If your bread slices are small, you may need 6 slices instead of 4.*

CHEF'S NOTE: *For a gluten-free option, make certain to use certified gluten-free tofu, gluten-free vegan cheese and gluten-free bread in this recipe.*

Preheat the oven to 200 degrees F. Line a small baking sheet with unbleached parchment paper. Put the tofu into a medium-sized bowl and mash with a potato masher or large fork until crumbly. Add the vegan cheese, turmeric, tamari, salt and pepper. Mash together until the tofu resembles the texture of cooked scrambled eggs.

Put a bread slice on a cutting board. Cut a hole in the center of the bread, about 3 inches in diameter, using a knife or cookie cutter. Spread a bit of vegan buttery spread on each side of the bread. Repeat with the remaining bread slices. (Reserve the bread "middles" to make bread crumbs for another meal.) Put 2 of the bread slices into a large, nonstick skillet over medium-low heat and let them begin to cook for 30 seconds to 1 minute on one side.

Scoop up one-quarter of the tofu mixture and place it in the center of each bread slice in the skillet, patting it down gently with a spatula until the filling becomes compact. Cook for 2 to 3 minutes and then carefully flip. Cover and cook for 5 to 7 minutes, or until the bread is golden and the tofu mixture is set. Transfer the cooked "toast" to the lined baking sheet and keep warm in the oven while cooking the other bread slices. Serve *Maple Roasted Portobello "Bacon"* (page 36) and fresh fruit on the side, if desired.

See photo of this recipe on page 30.

This recipe is from *Laura Theodore's Jazzy Vegetarian Classics: Vegan Twists on American Family Favorites (BenBella Books, 2013).* Reprinted with permission. Learn more at www.benbellabooks.com.

Rocky Mountain Toast *(page 29), above* Vegan Spinach, Onion and Red Pepper Crustless Quiche *(page 31), below*

GLUTEN-FREE

Creating a dairy-free, egg-free *and* gluten-free quiche can be challenging, but this flavorful version is so yummy you won't miss the cream, eggs or crust. This dish is perfect to serve for breakfast, lunch or light supper, plus it makes a festive holiday brunch entrée to please everyone!

VEGAN SPINACH, ONION & RED PEPPER *Crustless Quiche*

MAKES 6 SERVINGS

- **1 teaspoon vegan buttery spread, for coating dish**
- **1 block** (14 to 16 ounces) **extra-firm regular tofu, drained** (see note)
- **3 tablespoons unsweetened nondairy milk**
- **2 teaspoons gluten-free tamari**
- **2 teaspoons extra-virgin olive oil**
- **1 teaspoon ground turmeric**
- **¼ teaspoon smoked paprika**
- **1½ cups diced sweet onion**
- **1 cup seeded and sliced sweet mini peppers**
- **¾ cup shredded vegan cheese** (see note)
- **¼ cup minced fresh flat leaf parsley**
- **4 cups lightly packed baby spinach**
- **¼ teaspoon sweet paprika**

Preheat the oven to 350 degrees F. Generously coat a 9- to 10- inch round quiche dish or cake pan with vegan buttery spread. Put the tofu, nondairy milk, tamari, olive oil, turmeric and smoked paprika into a blender and process for about 30 seconds, until smooth. Transfer the mixture to a large mixing bowl.

Add the onion, peppers, vegan cheese and parsley and gently stir to combine. Fold in the baby spinach. Transfer the mixture to the prepared dish. Sprinkle the top with the sweet paprika. Bake for 30 to 35 minutes, or until the quiche is set and starts to crack (see note). Put the dish on a wire rack and gently loosen the sides of the quiche, using a kitchen knife. Let cool for 20 minutes before *carefully* slicing into 6 wedges (quiche will be quite soft). Serve warm with a crisp salad on the side, or refrigerate for 4 to 6 hours and serve cold (quiche will firm up more, once cold). Tightly covered and stored in the refrigerator, leftover quiche will keep up to 2 days.

CHEF'S NOTE: *Depending upon the type of vegan cheese you use, you may need to bake the quiche longer, up to 45 or 50 minutes.*

CHEF'S NOTE: *If you are cooking gluten free, make certain to purchase certified gluten-free tofu and gluten-free vegan cheese, available in most supermarkets.*

GLUTEN-FREE OPTION

This zesty scramble flawlessly takes the place of eggs for a satisfying morning meal. Served in crisp tortilla bowls, this dish makes a festive and filling breakfast entrée any day of the week.

TOFU-ZUCCHINI *Scramble* IN TORTILLA BOWLS

MAKES 4 SERVINGS

- **½ medium sweet onion, chopped**
- **2 tablespoons water, plus more as needed**
- **3½ teaspoons extra-virgin olive oil, divided**
- **3 teaspoons gluten-free tamari, divided**
- **1 teaspoon chili powder**
- **1 medium zucchini, cubed**
- **1 block** (14 to 16 ounces) **extra-firm regular tofu, drained** (see notes)
- **½ teaspoon ground turmeric**
- **½ teaspoon garlic powder**
- **⅛ teaspoon cayenne pepper**
- **½ cup shredded vegan cheese** (optional, see note)
- **1½ cups thinly sliced romaine lettuce**
- **1 medium avocado, peeled, pitted and sliced**
- **4 heaping tablespoons prepared salsa, plus more for serving**
- **4 *Tasty Tortilla Bowls*** (optional, page 37)

CHEF'S NOTE: *For a gluten-free option, make certain to use certified gluten-free tofu, gluten-free vegan cheese and make the tortilla bowls using gluten-free tortillas.*

Put the onion, water, 1 teaspoon olive oil, 1 teaspoon tamari and chili powder in a large skillet. Cover and cook, stirring occasionally, over medium heat for 3 to 4 minutes, or until the onion begins to become translucent. Add 2 tablespoons of water at a time as needed if the pan becomes dry. Add the zucchini, cover and cook 3 to 4 minutes, or until the zucchini begins to soften.

Meanwhile, as the onion and zucchini cook, put the tofu, 2 teaspoons olive oil, 2 teaspoons tamari, turmeric, garlic powder and cayenne pepper in a medium-sized bowl and mash with a potato masher or large fork until the mixture resembles the texture of cooked scrambled eggs. Add ½ teaspoon olive oil to the skillet and add the tofu mixture.

Decrease the heat to medium-low, cover and cook, stirring occasionally, until the scramble is heated through and lightly browned around the edges. Scatter the optional vegan cheese over the top, cover and cook 2 to 3 minutes, stirring occasionally. Turn off the heat and let the scramble stand for 2 minutes.

To serve, (see note) put a tortilla bowl on each of four salad plates. Put one-quarter of the romaine in the bottom of each tortilla bowl. Add one-quarter of the scramble to each. Arrange several avocado slices over the top of the scramble in each bowl, and top with 1 heaping tablespoon of salsa. Serve immediately, with more salsa served on the side.

CHEF'S NOTE: *This scramble also stands up well on its own, sans the tortilla bowls, with whole-grain toast served on the side.*

GLUTEN-FREE

If you've been missing scrambled eggs, then this is the dish for you. For a hearty breakfast, serve this scramble with whole-grain toast or *Yummy Banana-Oat Pancakes* (page 21) with *Maple Roasted Portobello "Bacon"* (page 36) and fresh fruit on the side. When I serve this dish family-style, I spoon the hot scramble into a covered serving tureen so it stays warm at the table.

NO-EGG TOFU-VEGGIE Scramble

MAKES 2 TO 3 SERVINGS

- **1 small sweet onion, chopped**
- **2 tablespoons extra-virgin olive oil, divided, plus more as needed**
- **5 to 6 ounces cremini or white button mushrooms, sliced**
- **½ large red or orange sweet bell pepper, seeded and chopped**
- **2 teaspoons gluten-free tamari, divided**
- **⅔ block** (about 10 ounces) **firm or extra-firm regular tofu, drained** (see note)
- **½ rounded teaspoon ground turmeric**
- **⅛ teaspoon cayenne pepper** (optional)
- **⅛ teaspoon sea salt, plus more as needed**
- **½ cup grated vegan cheese** (optional, see note)
- **Freshly ground black pepper, to taste**

Put the onion and 1 tablespoon oil into a large skillet. Cook over medium heat, stirring occasionally, until slightly softened, about 5 minutes. Add the mushrooms and cook, stirring occasionally, for 1 minute. Decrease the heat to medium-low. Add the peppers and 1 teaspoon of tamari. Cover and cook, stirring occasionally, for about 10 minutes until the onion is slightly golden. Add more oil or a bit of water if the pan becomes dry.

Meanwhile, put the tofu in a medium-sized bowl and mash with a potato masher or large fork until crumbly. Add the turmeric, optional cayenne, salt, 1 tablespoon olive oil and 1 teaspoon tamari. Mash until the tofu resembles the texture of cooked scrambled eggs.

Increase the heat to medium. Add the tofu to the skillet, adding a bit more oil (or water) if the pan becomes dry. Cook, stirring frequently, until the scramble is heated through and the tofu is lightly browned on the edges. Scatter the optional vegan cheese over the top and season with pepper to taste. Cover the skillet tightly, remove from the heat and let the vegan cheese melt for 4 to 5 minutes. Season with more salt, if desired. Serve immediately.

CHEF'S NOTE: *If you are cooking gluten-free, make certain to purchase certified gluten-free tofu and gluten-free vegan cheese, available in most supermarkets.*

These spicy *and* sweet portobello mushroom slices make the perfect breakfast side dish or topping for a crisp, green luncheon salad. They also make a yummy vegan BLT sandwich.

MAPLE ROASTED PORTOBELLO "Bacon"

MAKES 2 TO 4 SERVINGS

4 medium portobello mushrooms, de-stemmed and thinly sliced
1½ tablespoons gluten-free tamari
1½ tablespoons extra-virgin olive oil
1 tablespoon maple syrup
1¼ teaspoons smoked paprika
¼ heaping teaspoon garlic powder

Preheat the oven to 375 degrees F. Line a large, rimmed baking pan with unbleached parchment paper.

Put the mushroom slices, tamari, olive oil, maple syrup, paprika and garlic powder in a medium-sized bowl and toss gently with a large spoon to thoroughly coat. Transfer the mushroom mixture to the prepared pan and arrange in a single, even layer.

Bake for 20 to 35 minutes, or until the mushrooms are soft and lightly browned around the edges. Put the pan on a wire rack and let cool for 10 minutes before serving.

GLUTEN-FREE OPTION

Delightfully crunchy and fun to eat, whole-grain tortillas make wonderful edible bowls for serving everything from salads to stir-fries to a tofu scramble (page 34). You can even serve a hearty chili (page 199) in these tasty bowls!

TASTY *Tortilla* BOWLS

MAKES 4 BOWLS

4 vegan whole-grain tortillas or vegan gluten-free tortillas (each 10 to 11-inches in diameter)

Preheat the oven to 350 degrees F. Gently press one tortilla into a 5- to 6-inch round, oven-safe bowl (see photo). Repeat with the remaining 3 tortillas. Put the bowls on a rimmed baking pan. Bake the tortilla bowls for 7 to 10 minutes, or until crisp and golden around the edges. Put the pan on a wire rack to cool tortilla bowls before serving.

Tofu-Zucchini Scramble served in *Tasty Tortilla Bowls* (page 32).

A home-baked delight makes the quintessential mid-morning pick-me-up or afternoon snack. Nothin' like a freshly baked muffin to accompany a piping hot bowl of soup, warm quick bread to serve alongside a crisp green luncheon salad, a scrumptious slice of coffee cake to pair with your morning "cup of Joe" or a fruity oatmeal square to savor for a nutritious snack. No matter what the occasion, these vegan goodies will dazzle and delight everyone, no matter when you serve 'em!

CHAPTER FOUR

Baked Goodies

Lemony Maple-Cranberry Muffins, *page 48*

These yummy muffins offer a sweet surprise when you take your first bite. Perfect for a lunch-box or on-the-go snack, these gems hold a dollop of strawberry jam in the center to keep them nice and moist. So delicious!

STRAWBERRY SURPRISE *Muffins*

MAKES 12 MUFFINS

- 2 tablespoons golden flaxseeds
- 2 cups whole wheat flour, plus more as needed (see note for gluten-free option)
- ½ cup unsweetened shredded dried coconut
- 1 tablespoon baking powder
- 1 cup raw cane turbinado sugar, vegan cane sugar or your preferred dry sweetener
- 1¼ teaspoons ground cinnamon
- ½ teaspoon sea salt
- 1⅔ cups plus 1 tablespoon unsweetened nondairy milk, plus more as needed
- 3 tablespoons extra-virgin olive oil
- 12 rounded teaspoons of seedless (or seeded) strawberry jam or preserves

Preheat the oven to 350 degrees F. Line a 12-cup standard muffin tin with paper liners. Put the flaxseeds into a high-performance blending appliance and process into a fine flour. Put the ground flaxseeds, whole wheat flour, coconut and baking powder into a large bowl and stir with a dry whisk until combined. Add the sugar, cinnamon and sea salt and stir with the whisk until thoroughly combined.

Make a well in the middle of the dry ingredients and add the nondairy milk and olive oil. Stir with a large spoon to combine. If the mixture seems a bit dry, add 1 more tablespoon of nondairy milk. Alternately, if the mixture seems too wet, add 1 more tablespoon of flour.

Fill each prepared muffin cup one-half full with the batter. Make a small well in the center with a spoon or your finger. Spoon 1 rounded teaspoon of strawberry jam into the well. Top with the remaining batter, distributing it evenly among the muffin cups.

Bake for 25 to 30 minutes, or until a toothpick inserted into the side of a muffin comes out clean.

Put the muffin tin on a wire rack and let cool at least 15 minutes before serving. Serve warm or at room temperature. Covered tightly and stored in the refrigerator, leftover muffins will keep for about 2 days.

CHEF'S NOTE: *For a gluten-free option, use a "1-to-1" variety of gluten-free flour in place of the whole wheat flour, adding an additional 3 to 5 minutes to the baking time if needed.*

Light and airy, with a pop of fresh juicy blueberries, these muffins make an excellent addition to just about any meal. Vegan "buttermilk" helps them to rise and keeps them moist. These beauties make a snazzy snack but are sweet enough to serve for dessert, too.

Blueberry "BUTTERMILK" MUFFINS

MAKES 18 MUFFINS

1½ cups unsweetened nondairy milk, plus more as needed

¼ cup freshly squeezed lemon juice

⅓ cup extra-virgin olive oil

1½ cups whole wheat flour

½ cup gluten-free, quick cooking rolled oats

1½ teaspoons baking powder

½ teaspoon baking soda

1 cup vegan cane sugar

2 cups fresh blueberries

Preheat the oven to 350 degrees F. Line three 6-cup standard muffin tins with paper liners. To make the vegan "buttermilk," put the nondairy milk and lemon juice into a small pitcher or bowl and stir to combine. Let stand for 5 to 10 minutes. Stir in the olive oil.

To make the batter, put the flour, oats, baking powder and baking soda into a large bowl and stir with a dry whisk to combine. Add the sugar and stir with the whisk to thoroughly combine. Fold the blueberries into the flour mixture. Make a well in the center of the flour mixture and add the vegan "buttermilk." Stir to combine. The batter will be quite thick, but if it seems overly dry, stir in a bit more nondairy milk, 1 tablespoon at a time, until the mixture is moist.

Mound the mixture into the prepared muffin cups. Bake for 25 to 27 minutes or until a toothpick inserted into the middle of a muffin comes out clean. Put the muffin tins on wire racks and let cool at least 30 minutes before serving. Covered tightly and stored in the refrigerator, leftover muffins will keep for 3 to 4 days.

These moist muffins are like eating peach pie—all wrapped up in a muffin! This easy-to-assemble goody makes a perfect breakfast treat, afternoon snack or sweet dessert.

Southern Peach PECAN MUFFINS

MAKES 12 MUFFINS

- 2 cups whole wheat flour
- 2 teaspoons baking powder
- 1 teaspoon ground cinnamon
- 1 cup vegan dark brown sugar, firmly packed
- 1 cup unsweetened nondairy milk
- ⅓ cup extra-virgin olive oil
- 1¼ teaspoons vanilla extract
- 1 cup peach purée (from 2 to 3 medium-large peaches, see note)
- ¾ cup chopped pecans
- ½ cup dark raisins

CHEF'S NOTE: *To make the peach purée, peel, pit and chop 2 to 3 peaches. Transfer to a blender and process on low into a thick purée, being careful not to liquefy.*

Preheat the oven to 375 degrees F. Line a 12-cup standard muffin tin with paper liners. Put the flour, baking powder and cinnamon into a large bowl and stir with a dry whisk to combine. Add the brown sugar and stir with the whisk to combine. Make a well in the center of the dry ingredients.

Add the nondairy milk, olive oil and vanilla extract and stir with a large spoon until thoroughly combined. Add in the peach purée and stir to combine. Fold in the pecans and raisins and stir to combine. Mound the mixture into the prepared muffin cups. Bake for 25 to 27 minutes or until a toothpick inserted into the center of a muffin comes out clean. Put the muffin tin on a wire rack and let cool at least 15 minutes before serving. Serve warm or at room temperature. Covered tightly and stored in the refrigerator, leftover muffins will keep for about 2 days.

With minimal ingredients required, these semi-sweet, tasty, plant-based treats whip up fast and are ideal for an afternoon snack or nutritious dessert.

Coconut CHOCOLATE CHIP MUFFINS

MAKES 6 MUFFINS

1½ cups whole wheat pastry flour (see note)

½ cup unsweetened shredded dried coconut

1 teaspoon baking soda

1 teaspoon baking powder

¼ teaspoon sea salt

½ cup firmly packed vegan brown sugar or cane sugar

1 cup plus 2 tablespoons sweetened nondairy milk

2 teaspoons freshly squeezed lemon juice

½ cup vegan dark chocolate chips

Preheat the oven to 375 degrees F. Line a 6-cup standard muffin tin with paper liners. Put the flour, coconut, baking soda, baking powder and salt in a large bowl and stir with a dry whisk to combine. Add the brown sugar and stir with the whisk to combine. Make a well in the center of the dry ingredients and stir in the nondairy milk and the lemon juice. Stir in the chocolate chips.

Mound the mixture into the prepared muffin cups. Bake for 25 to 35 minutes, or until golden and a toothpick inserted in the middle of a muffin comes out clean. Put the muffin tin on a wire rack and let cool at least 15 minutes before serving. Serve warm or at room temperature. Covered tightly and stored in the refrigerator, leftover muffins will keep for about 2 days.

CHEF'S NOTE: *You may use regular whole wheat flour in this recipe. The muffins will be a bit more dense in texture.*

Photos courtesy of Annie Olivero. Learn more about Annie on page 296.

This recipe is from *Laura Theodore's Jazzy Vegetarian Classics: Vegan Twists on American Family Favorites (BenBella Books, 2013).* Reprinted with permission. Learn more at www.benbellabooks.com.

With the tangy taste of lemon and dried cranberries, enhanced with sweet maple syrup and toasted wheat germ, this lovely muffin is totally tasty!

Lemony MAPLE-CRANBERRY MUFFINS

MAKES 12 MUFFINS

2 teaspoons vegan buttery spread, for coating muffin cups

1¼ cups unsweetened nondairy milk

¼ cup freshly squeezed lemon juice (from about 2 medium lemons; zest the lemons first, before squeezing)

2 cups whole wheat flour

⅓ cup toasted wheat germ

1½ teaspoons baking powder

½ teaspoon baking soda

¼ teaspoon sea salt

½ teaspoon lemon zest

⅔ cup firmly packed vegan dark brown sugar

¼ cup maple syrup

¼ cup water

1 tablespoon extra-virgin olive oil

½ cup sweetened dried cranberries, plus more, if desired, to top muffins

Preheat the oven to 375 degrees F. Liberally coat a 12-cup standard muffin tin with vegan buttery spread. Put the nondairy milk and the lemon juice into a small bowl or pitcher to make a light vegan "buttermilk." Let stand while preparing the batter.

To make the batter, put the flour, wheat germ, baking powder, baking soda and salt into a large bowl and stir with a dry whisk until combined. Add the lemon zest and stir with the whisk to combine. Add the brown sugar and briskly whisk to combine. (There will be little flecks of the brown sugar still visible in the flour mixture, but that is fine). Make a well in the center of the dry ingredients and add the maple syrup, water, olive oil and nondairy milk/lemon mixture and stir with a large spoon to combine. Fold the cranberries into the batter.

Divide the batter evenly among the 12 muffin cups. If desired, you can top each muffin with 3 to 4 more cranberries, gently pushing them into the top of the muffins so the cranberries adhere while baking. Bake for 25 minutes, or until a toothpick inserted into the center of a muffin comes out clean. Put the muffin tin on a wire rack and loosen the sides of the muffins with a knife. Let cool for 10 minutes. Carefully remove the muffins and put them directly on the wire rack. Let cool 5 minutes more and serve warm or at room temperature. Covered tightly and stored in the refrigerator, leftover muffins will keep for about 3 days.

If you want to serve homemade bread for breakfast, lunch or dinner, but are short on time, this soda bread is the perfect solution. With its thick, chewy crust and crumbly moist texture inside, no one will ever suspect it took only 15 minutes to prepare for the oven!

Petite SODA BREAD

MAKES 1 SMALL LOAF, ABOUT 4 SERVINGS

- ½ cup plus 1 tablespoon water, plus more as needed
- ½ cup unsweetened nondairy milk
- 2 teaspoons freshly squeezed lemon juice
- 2 cups plus 4 teaspoons whole wheat flour, divided
- 1 teaspoon baking soda
- ¼ teaspoon sea salt
- ¼ cup sweetened dried cranberries (see note)
- ¼ cup raisins

Preheat the oven to 450 degrees F. Line a pizza pan with unbleached parchment paper. Put the water, nondairy milk and lemon juice in a small bowl and stir to combine. Let the mixture stand for 5 to 10 minutes to make a light vegan "buttermilk."

Meanwhile, put 2 cups flour, baking soda and salt in a large bowl and stir with a dry whisk to combine. Pour the "buttermilk" into the dry mixture and stir with a large spoon to combine, forming a soft dough. Gently fold in the cranberries and raisins. Do not overmix. Turn the dough out onto a surface dusted with 3 teaspoons of flour. Lightly knead for 30 seconds or so. Avoid overworking the dough.

Shape the dough into a round disk-shaped loaf and gently place it on the prepared pan. Sprinkle the remaining 1 teaspoon of flour over the top of the loaf. Cut a deep "X" in the top with a sharp knife. Bake for 10 minutes. Decrease the oven temperature to 400 degrees F and bake for another 25 to 30 minutes, or until the top is firm and crusty. Put the bread on a wire rack to cool for 10 to 15 minutes before slicing. Serve warm.

CHEF'S NOTE: *You may use just dried cranberries, or just raisins in this recipe, if you prefer. Alternately, you can omit the cranberries and raisins altogether, if desired.*

Yes, we have some bananas! This bread is so *banana-y* that I *had* to include the word "banana" twice in the recipe title. It's easy to prepare, moist *and* delicious.

Banana, BANANA BREAD

MAKES 10 SERVINGS

- 1 teaspoon vegan buttery spread, for coating loaf pan
- ¾ cup plus 5 tablespoons sweetened or unsweetened nondairy milk
- 2 tablespoons freshly squeezed lemon juice
- 2 cups plus 2 tablespoons whole wheat flour
- 1 teaspoon baking soda
- 1 cup vegan cane sugar
- ⅓ cup extra-virgin olive oil
- 1 teaspoon vanilla extract
- 1½ cups peeled and mashed ripe bananas (from 4 small or 3 medium)
- 1 cup chopped walnuts

Preheat the oven to 375 degrees F. Lightly coat a 9- x 5-inch loaf pan with vegan buttery spread. Line the lengthwise sides and bottom of the pan with unbleached parchment paper, leaving an overhang of 2-inch "wings" on the two long sides of the pan. Put the nondairy milk and lemon juice into a small pitcher or bowl and stir to combine. Let stand for 5 to 10 minutes to make a light vegan "buttermilk."

Put the flour, baking soda and sugar in a large bowl and stir with a dry whisk until combined. Add the lemon/nondairy milk mixture, olive oil, vanilla and mashed bananas and stir with a large spoon to combine. Fold in the chopped walnuts.

Pour the batter into the prepared loaf pan. Bake for 45 minutes. Decrease the heat to 350 degrees F and bake for an additional 15 to 20 minutes or until the top of the loaf is golden and a toothpick inserted into the center of the loaf comes out clean. Put the pan on a wire rack and let cool for 5 minutes. Using the parchment paper "wings," carefully lift the bread from the pan and put it on the wire rack. Carefully peel back the paper from the sides of the bread and let cool an additional 1 hour before slicing. Serve warm, or wrap tightly, refrigerate and serve cold. Wrapped tightly and stored in the refrigerator, leftover bread will keep for 3 days.

A yummy layer of apples tops this tasty cake that's filled with good foods like bananas, coconut and sweet dates. It's the perfect snack to complement hot tea or a dark cup o' joe.

APPLE 'N DATE Coffee Cake

MAKES 6 SERVINGS

APPLE LAYER

2 medium apples, cored and cut into small chunks (do not peel)

1 tablespoon vegan brown sugar or your preferred dry sweetener

1 tablespoon maple syrup

CAKE

2 medium ripe bananas, peeled

1 tablespoon maple syrup

1 cup whole wheat flour

⅓ cup unsweetened shredded dried coconut

¼ cup vegan brown sugar or your preferred dry sweetener

1 teaspoon baking powder

½ cup pitted and diced Medjool dates

⅔ cup water

Preheat the oven to 375 degrees F. Line the bottom of a 9-inch round cake pan with unbleached parchment paper. To make the apple layer, put the apples, 1 tablespoon brown sugar and 1 tablespoon maple syrup into a medium-sized bowl and stir until the apples are evenly coated. Transfer to the prepared pan, spreading the apples in an even layer.

To make the cake batter, put the bananas and maple syrup into a medium-sized bowl and mash into a chunky purée using a potato masher or large fork. Put the flour, coconut, ¼ cup brown sugar and baking powder into a large bowl and stir with a dry whisk to combine. Stir in the banana mixture, dates and water and mix just until incorporated. Pour the batter over the apples in the pan and smooth the top.

Bake for 40 to 50 minutes, or until golden and a toothpick inserted into the center of the cake comes out clean. Put the pan on a wire rack and loosen the sides with a knife. Let cool for 10 to 12 minutes. Invert onto a serving platter and carefully peel off the parchment paper. Let cool for 5 minutes more before slicing. Serve warm or room temperature. Wrapped tightly and stored in the refrigerator, leftover cake will keep for about 3 days.

See photo of this recipe on page 54.

Apple 'n Date Coffee Cake *(page 53), above*

Chocolate Chip Oatmeal Bread *(page 55), below*

Need a treat, but want it to be filling, too? This lively bread makes a nutritious indulgence when you're seeking something sweet, but you want health benefits, too! With a pop of chocolate nestled in a batter of whole wheat flour, rolled oats, sunflower seeds and raisins, this quick bread will truly satisfy.

Chocolate Chip-OATMEAL BREAD

MAKES 12 SLICES

- 1 teaspoon vegan buttery spread, for coating pan
- 1½ cups whole wheat flour
- 1 cup plus 1½ tablespoons old fashioned rolled oats, divided
- 2 teaspoons baking powder
- ⅓ cup vegan cane sugar
- ½ teaspoon ground cinnamon
- ½ cup raisins
- ⅓ cup vegan dark chocolate chips (55%, 70% *or* 85% cacao)
- ⅓ cup raw unsalted sunflower seeds
- 1½ cups unsweetened nondairy milk, plus more as needed

CHEF'S NOTE: *If desired, you can add 1 tablespoon chocolate chips and 1 tablespoon sunflower seeds to the top of the loaf after the bread bakes for about 35 minutes.*

Preheat the oven to 375 degrees F. Lightly coat an 8- x 4-inch loaf pan with vegan buttery spread. Line the lengthwise sides and bottom of the pan with unbleached parchment paper, leaving an overhang of 2-inch "wings" on the two long sides of the pan. Put the whole wheat flour, 1 cup rolled oats and baking powder into a large bowl and stir with a dry whisk to combine.

Add the sugar and cinnamon and stir with the whisk to combine. Stir in the raisins, chocolate chips and sunflower seeds and mix with a large spoon to combine. Add the nondairy milk and stir until well blended, adding a bit more nondairy milk if the mixture seems dry. Batter will be thick. Spoon the batter into the prepared loaf pan, smoothing the top with a rubber spatula.

Sprinkle 1½ tablespoons of rolled oats evenly over the top of the bread (see note). Bake for 40 to 45 minutes, or until the top of the bread is firm, slightly golden and a toothpick inserted in the center of the bread comes out clean. Put the bread on a wire rack and let cool for 5 minutes. Using the parchment paper "wings," carefully lift the bread from the pan and put it on the wire rack. Carefully peel back the paper from the sides of the bread and let cool an additional 30 minutes before slicing. Serve warm, or wrap tightly, refrigerate and serve cold. Wrapped tightly and stored in the refrigerator, leftover bread will keep for 3 days.

Photo courtesy of Annie Olivero. Learn more about Annie on page 296.

Just a few basic ingredients come together to make up these scrumptious cookie squares that do triple duty as a healthy dessert, afternoon snack or bountiful breakfast treat.

Raspberry OAT SQUARES

MAKES 12 TO 16 SQUARES

- 2 very large ripe bananas, peeled
- 2 tablespoons maple syrup
- 2 cups gluten-free, quick cooking rolled oats
- ⅓ cup sweetened dried cranberries
- ¼ cup unsweetened shredded dried coconut
- ½ cup plus 2 tablespoons raspberry preserves

Preheat the oven to 375 degrees F. Line the bottom of an 8-inch square rimmed baking pan with unbleached parchment paper, leaving an overhang of 2-inch "wings" on two sides of the pan. Put the bananas and maple syrup in a large bowl and mash into a chunky purée using a potato masher or large fork. Stir in the oats, cranberries and coconut.

Spread half of the oat mixture in an even layer in the prepared pan. Spread the raspberry preserves in an even layer over the oat mixture. Spread the remaining oat mixture in an even layer over the preserves. Bake for 25 to 30 minutes or until slightly golden. Put the pan on a wire rack and let cool 3 minutes. Using the paper "wings," carefully lift the squares out of the pan and set them on the wire rack. Let cool 15 minutes.

Lifting with the paper "wings," transfer the squares to a cutting board and slice into 12 to 16 squares, using a serrated knife and wiping the knife clean after cutting each row of squares. Let cool 20 minutes before serving, or loosely cover, refrigerate for 2 to 3 hours and serve cold. Stored in an airtight container in the refrigerator, leftover squares will keep for 3 days.

This yummy dessert is both healthy and delicious, featuring luscious peach preserves and sweet dates, to give it a little bit of a southern flair.

Peachy DATE NUT BARS

MAKES 12 BARS

- 2 very large ripe bananas, peeled
- 2 tablespoons maple syrup
- 2 cups gluten-free, quick cooking rolled oats
- ½ cup chopped pecans
- 8 to 10 Medjool dates, diced
- ½ teaspoon ground cinnamon
- ¾ cup peach preserves

Preheat the oven to 375 degrees F. Line the bottom of an 8-inch square rimmed baking pan with unbleached parchment paper, leaving an overhang of 2-inch "wings" on two sides of the pan. Put the bananas and maple syrup in a large bowl and mash into a chunky purée using a potato masher or large fork. Stir in the oats, pecans, dates and cinnamon.

Spread half of the oat mixture in an even layer in the prepared pan. Spread the peach preserves in an even layer over the oat mixture. Spread the remaining oat mixture in an even layer over the preserves. Bake for 25 to 30 minutes or until slightly golden. Put the pan on a wire rack and let cool 3 minutes. Using the paper "wings," carefully lift the squares out of the pan and set them on the wire rack. Let cool 15 minutes.

Lifting with the paper "wings," transfer the bars to a cutting board and slice into 12 bars, using a serrated knife and wiping the knife clean after cutting each row of bars. Let cool 20 minutes before serving, or loosely cover, refrigerate for 2 to 3 hours and serve cold. Stored in an airtight container in the refrigerator, leftover bars will keep for 3 days.

JAZZY TIP: *I like using unbleached parchment paper, which makes any pan nonstick and makes cleanup much speedier. Plus, it's compostable! I opt for unbleached parchment paper because it is chlorine-free—better for my family and better for the environment.*

Tasty appetizers make the perfect start to any plant-based meal. Whetting guests' palates with various tempting tapas is an ideal way to get the party going! Delectable dips, tiny bites, appealing hors d'oeuvres and a refreshing drink all come together here to provide you with a welcome way to start your meal. The recipes in this chapter *all* make great snacks, too!

CHAPTER FIVE

Tasty Starters

Lemony Guacamole, *page 64*

A pop of turmeric adds jazz to this flavorful, creamy and easy-to-prepare hummus.

TURMERIC-LEMON *Hummus*

MAKES 4 SERVINGS

1 can (14 to 16 ounces) **chickpeas** (garbanzo beans), **drained and rinsed**

2 tablespoons freshly squeezed lemon juice, plus more as needed

1 tablespoon sesame tahini (purchase certified gluten-free tahini if you are gluten-free)

1 tablespoon water, plus more as needed

1 small clove garlic, chopped

½ teaspoon ground cumin

½ teaspoon chili powder

¼ teaspoon ground turmeric

¼ teaspoon sea salt

⅛ teaspoon cayenne pepper

Parsley sprig (optional, for garnish)

Put all of the ingredients into a blender or food processor and process until smooth. Add a bit more lemon (to taste) or water as needed to achieve desired consistency. Transfer to a serving bowl and garnish with a parsley sprig, if desired. Served with veggie sticks, this hummus makes a wonderful appetizer platter.

GLUTEN-FREE

This is the dip to serve when you are looking to impress non-vegans. The cashews and beans combine to produce a creamy, "cheese-y" texture. Freshly squeezed lemon juice and a hint of cayenne pepper add pizzazz to this crowd-pleasing recipe.

Cheeze-y CASHEW DIP

MAKES 6 TO 8 SERVINGS

- **1 can** (14 to 16 ounces) **white beans** (any variety), **drained and rinsed**
- **¼ cup raw cashews**
- **2 tablespoons water**
- **1 tablespoon plus 1 teaspoon freshly squeezed lemon juice**
- **1 clove garlic, chopped or ¼ teaspoon garlic powder**
- **½ teaspoon sea salt**
- **¼ teaspoon cayenne pepper**
- **2 tablespoons seeded and diced red or orange sweet bell pepper** (plus more for garnish, optional)
- **Parsley sprig (optional, for garnish)**

Put the white beans, cashews, water, lemon juice, garlic, salt and cayenne pepper in a blender or food processor and process until smooth and creamy. Transfer to a pretty bowl and fold in the optional diced pepper. Garnish with a parsley sprig and more diced pepper, if desired, and serve.

GLUTEN-FREE

Just a few ingredients whip together in five minutes to make this appetizing avocado dip.

Lemony GUACAMOLE

MAKES 4 SERVINGS

2 medium avocados, peeled, pitted and rough chopped

1 small clove garlic, minced or scant ⅛ teaspoon garlic powder

1 tablespoon freshly squeezed lemon juice, plus more to taste

¼ teaspoon sea salt

Dash cayenne pepper, to taste

Basil sprig (optional, for garnish)

Put the chopped avocado into a medium-sized bowl. Add the garlic, lemon juice, sea salt and cayenne pepper. Mix together using a potato masher or large fork, until smooth. Taste and add more lemon juice, if desired. Transfer to a serving bowl, garnish with optional basil sprig and serve. This makes a perfect, quick dip for veggie sticks or tortilla chips. It's also great for making avocado toast.

3 INGREDIENTS OR LESS

GLUTEN-FREE

This zingy guacamole is so easy to make! It's a real crowd-pleaser and I like to serve this dandy dip when hosting a casual get together.

SALSA-LICIOUS *Guacamole*

MAKES 4 SERVINGS

1 medium ripe avocado, pitted and peeled

⅓ cup mild, medium or hot salsa, plus more as needed

Parsley sprig (optional, for garnish)

Put the avocado and salsa in a bowl and mash with a potato masher or large fork, until well combined. Taste and add more salsa, if desired. Transfer to a pretty serving bowl, garnish with optional parsley and serve.

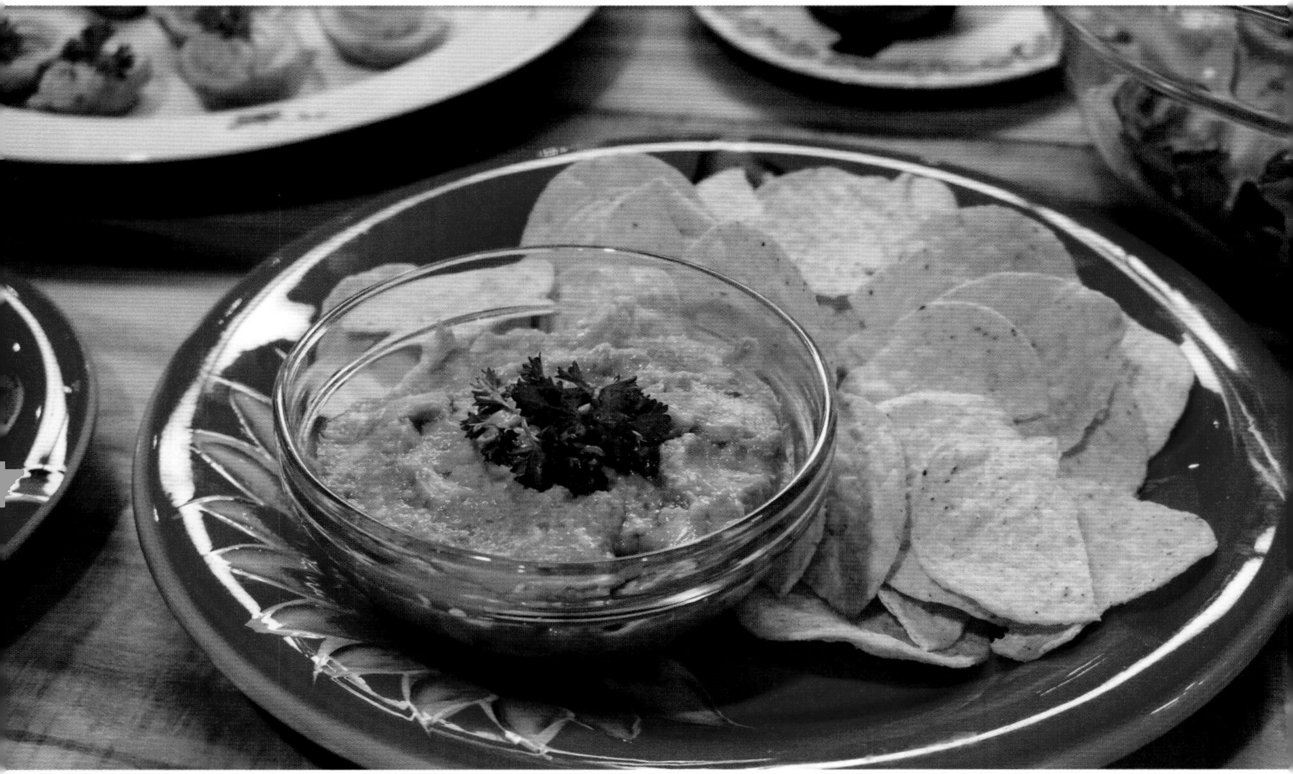

This delicious dip is truly a fan favorite! *Not* Liver is a satisfying appetizer year round, but it's particularly inviting during the fall holidays. It truly mimics the texture and taste of the traditional pâté.

Jazzy Vegetarian NOT LIVER

MAKES 6 TO 8 SERVINGS

- **1 tablespoon extra-virgin olive oil, plus more as needed**
- **3 sweet onions, chopped**
- **1 can** (14 to 16 ounces) **sweet peas, drained**
- **¾ cup chopped walnuts**
- **⅓ block** (4 to 5 ounces) **firm or extra-firm regular tofu, drained and cubed** (see note)
- **2 tablespoons tomato paste**
- **¼ teaspoon sea salt**
- **Freshly ground black pepper, to taste**

Heat 1 tablespoon olive oil in a large skillet over medium-low heat. Add the onions and cook about 25 minutes, stirring occasionally, until very tender and lightly browned. Add more oil or water, 1 teaspoon at a time, as needed to prevent sticking. Let cool slightly.

Transfer to a food processor or high-performance blending appliance. Add the peas, walnuts, tofu, tomato paste and salt. Process until slightly chunky, stopping to scrape down the sides of the bowl as needed. (Depending on the size of your appliance, you may need to process the mixture in batches.) Season with pepper, to taste. Spoon the mixture into a serving bowl. Cover tightly and refrigerate for about 4 hours before serving to allow the flavors to blend. Tightly covered and stored in the refrigerator, the dip will keep for 2 days.

CHEF'S NOTE: *If you are cooking gluten free, make certain to purchase certified gluten-free tofu and tomato paste, available in most supermarkets.*

GLUTEN-FREE

This simple "sushi-like" roll uses zucchini instead of seaweed for the wrapper and is easy to prepare. The dipping sauce is super quick, too, but don't be fooled: the roll (once dipped in the sauce) is full of *umami* flavor.

ZUCCHINI-AVOCADO "Sushi Rolls" with Tamari-Scallion Dipping Sauce

MAKES 3 TO 4 SERVINGS (ABOUT 12 ROLLS TOTAL)

DIPPING SAUCE

3 tablespoons maple syrup

3 tablespoons gluten-free tamari

1 scallion, white *and* green parts, thinly sliced

ROLLS

2 medium zucchini

2 medium carrots, peeled and cut into *very* thin sticks

1 large avocado, peeled, pitted and thinly sliced

To make the dipping sauce, put the maple syrup and tamari in a small bowl and briskly whisk until combined. Pour the sauce into 3 or 4 tiny bowls and top with several scallion slices.

To make the rolls, put each zucchini on a cutting board. Using a wide vegetable peeler or mandolin, carefully cut the zucchini into very thin, long slices (strips), making about 6 slices or so from each zucchini (about 12 slices in all). Cut the remaining zucchini into very thin sticks, about the same size as the carrot sticks.

Lay one zucchini slice on the cutting board and arrange several carrot sticks, zucchini sticks and a few slices of avocado at one end of the zucchini slice. Carefully roll up the zucchini slice around the avocado, carrot and zucchini sticks. Put the roll on a plate, seam side down. Continue in this manner until you have about 12 rolls. Serve 3 to 4 rolls per person, with dipping sauce on the side.

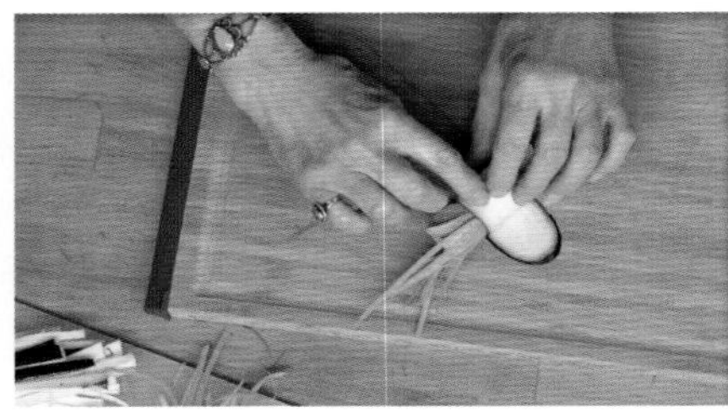

GLUTEN-FREE OPTION

My husband adores these little pizza squares! They make a real hit at any party you are hosting and can be served as an appetizer or as a main course offering. Change up the toppers with whatever your family likes, and you have a perfect weeknight meal for everyone!

FLATBREAD MINI-VEGGIE *Pizzas*

MAKES 8 TO 10 SERVINGS

- **2 rectangular** (about 16- x 6-inch or similarly sized) **store-bought, vegan flatbread-style pizza crusts** (see note)
- **1 to 2 tablespoons extra-virgin olive oil**
- **½ cup prepared vegan marinara sauce**
- **1 teaspoon Italian seasoning blend**
- **6 ounces cremini mushrooms, thinly sliced**
- **⅓ to ½ cup chopped green olives, with pimento**
- **8 ounces jarred fire roasted sweet red bell peppers, sliced**
- **½ cup shredded vegan cheese** (optional, see note)
- **8 to 12 fresh basil leaves, torn**

Preheat the oven to 425 degrees F. Line a large, rimmed baking sheet with unbleached parchment paper. Put the pizza crusts on the lined baking sheet. Brush *each* crust with a scant tablespoon of olive oil and then add ¼ cup marinara sauce over each crust and spread evenly. Sprinkle each crust with ½ teaspoon Italian seasoning. Arrange one-half of the mushrooms, olives, sliced peppers and optional vegan cheese evenly over each crust. Bake for 10 to 17 minutes (time in the oven depends upon the thickness of your crust), or until the crust is crisp and veggies are heated through. Put the sheet on a wire rack. Sprinkle the basil over the top of the pizzas and let cool 3 minutes. Transfer the pizzas to a cutting board and cut into squares. Arrange on a pretty platter and serve.

CHEF'S NOTE: *If you are cooking gluten free, make certain to purchase certified vegan, gluten-free pizza crusts (available in some supermarkets). Gluten-free vegan cheese and marinara sauce can be found in most supermarkets.*

Flatbread Mini-Veggie Pizzas prepared with optional vegan cheese (right).

GLUTEN-FREE

A sweet and spicy surprise awaits when you bite into these dainty and flavorful potato delights, dipped into a creamy, tangy sauce.

GARAM MASALA Sweet Potato BITES with Spicy Ketchup Dip

MAKES 4 TO 6 SERVINGS

SWEET POTATOES

3 large sweet potatoes or yams, peeled and cut into thin wedges

3 tablespoons maple syrup, plus more as needed

1 tablespoon garam masala

SPICY KETCHUP DIP

½ cup ketchup

1 teaspoon garam masala

Dash cayenne pepper

Preheat the oven to 350 degrees F. Line a large, rimmed baking pan with unbleached parchment paper.

Put the sweet potatoes, maple syrup and 1 tablespoon garam masala into a large bowl and stir with a large spoon to combine. Add an additional tablespoon of maple syrup if the sweet potatoes are still a bit dry. Arrange the potatoes in a single layer on the prepared baking pan. Bake for 50 to 70 minutes or until golden brown and slightly crisp.

To make the dip, put the ketchup, 1 teaspoon garam masala and a dash of cayenne pepper into a small bowl. Stir to combine. Cover and refrigerate until ready to serve.

When the potatoes are cooked, put the pan on a wire rack and let cool for 15 minutes. Arrange the sweet potato bites on a serving platter in a pleasing manner and serve with the dip on the side.

Tender and tasty, these enticing mushrooms are easy to prepare. With just a few simple ingredients, they make a yummy first course or light weeknight entrée.

Snazzy STUFFED MUSHROOMS

MAKES 3 TO 4 MAIN DISH SERVINGS OR 6 TO 8 APPETIZER SERVINGS

1½ tablespoons extra-virgin olive oil

16 ounces large, white button or cremini "stuffing" mushrooms, cleaned and stems removed

1 teaspoon gluten-free tamari, plus more as needed

1¼ cups lightly packed, vegan whole-grain (or vegan *and* gluten-free) **bread crumbs** (see notes)

3 tablespoons minced green olives, with pimento

2½ tablespoons finely minced sweet onion

1 teaspoon Italian seasoning blend

⅛ teaspoon sea salt

Freshly ground black pepper, to taste

2 tablespoons water, plus more as needed

CHEF'S NOTE: *To make fresh bread crumbs, tear 2 to 4 slices of fresh, soft whole-grain bread into chunks. Put the bread chunks into a blender and process (on low) into coarse crumbs.*

Preheat the oven to 400 degrees F. Line a 9- x 9-inch square rimmed baking pan with foil, and then line with unbleached parchment paper. Spread ½ tablespoon of olive oil over the parchment paper in an even layer, using a pastry brush or small spoon. Arrange the mushrooms cap side down on the prepared pan, gently rubbing them into the olive oil, so that some of the olive oil coats each mushroom cap. Sprinkle about 1/16 teaspoon of tamari over the gills of each mushroom.

Put the bread crumbs, olives, onion, Italian seasoning and salt in a small bowl and stir with a spoon to combine. Add 1 tablespoon of olive oil and stir until the crumbs are well coated with oil. Mound some stuffing into each mushroom cap, pressing it firmly into the cap. Top the stuffing with several grinds of freshly ground black pepper, if desired. Tent with foil and bake for 30 minutes. Remove the foil and add 2 tablespoons of water to the bottom of the pan. Bake uncovered for an additional 15 to 25 minutes or until the mushrooms are very soft and the stuffing is crisp, adding more water, to the *bottom* of the pan, 1 to 2 tablespoons at a time, if pan becomes dry. Put the pan on a wire rack and let cool 5 minutes before serving.

CHEF'S NOTE: *To make this recipe gluten free, use vegan, gluten-free bread to make your fresh bread crumbs.*

These cute little devils beautifully take the place of a classic stuffed egg.

VEGAN *Deviled* "EGGS"

MAKES 6 SERVINGS

10 to 12 "Pee-Wee' white potatoes or Dutch baby white potatoes, steamed (until fork tender) **and chilled**

1 container (10 to 12 ounces) **store-bought, prepared hummus** (any flavor) **or** ***Turmeric-Lemon Hummus*** (page 62) (see note)

Parsley sprigs (optional, for garnish)

Cut each steamed and chilled potato in half lengthwise. Hollow out a small cavity from each potato half with a melon baller, to resemble hard boiled egg halves. Pipe (or spoon) some hummus into each half. Garnish each with a parsley sprig, if desired. Arrange on a pretty platter and serve.

CHEF'S NOTE: *If you are gluten free and purchasing* store bought *hummus, make certain it's certified gluten free.*

GLUTEN-FREE

My mom often gave us celery sticks stuffed with cream cheese when I was a kid. Here are a few options to make this classic into a healthy plant-based snack or starter.

MOM'S *Stuffed* CELERY STICKS

MAKES 6 SERVINGS

12 large celery sticks, washed with tough ends trimmed

12 tablespoons nut or seed butter (almond, cashew, hazelnut, sunflower or peanut butter)

Spread a generous tablespoon of your favorite nut or seed butter (see note) into each celery stick. Arrange on a platter and serve.

VARIATIONS: *Substitute vegan cream cheese or your favorite hummus for the nut (or seed) butter.*

CHEF'S NOTE: *If you are gluten free, be certain to purchase certified gluten-free nut butters, vegan cream cheese and/or hummus.*

I like to serve this refreshing beverage to guests when they arrive for a casual summertime party.

BERRY MAPLE-MINT Iced Tea

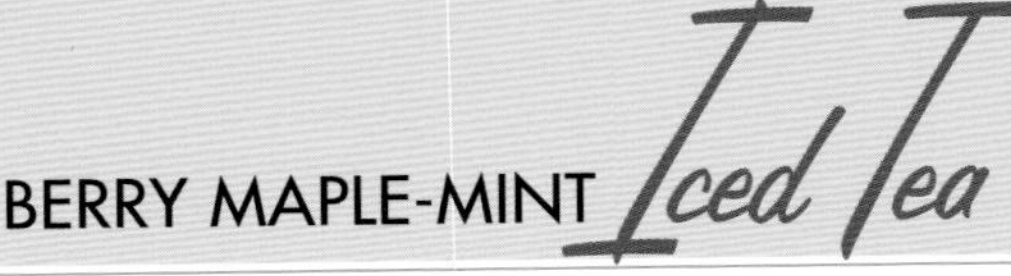

MAKES 4 TO 6 SERVINGS

- 4 berry-flavored tea bags (see note)
- 5½ cups water, divided
- 2 heaping tablespoons maple syrup, plus more to taste
- 4 to 6 fresh spearmint or peppermint sprigs
- Ice cubes

Bring 4½ cups of water to a boil over high heat in a large pot. Turn off the heat and add the tea bags. Cover and let steep for 1 hour. Remove the tea bags. Add the maple syrup and stir to incorporate. Taste and add more maple syrup, if desired.

Add the remaining 1 cup water and stir to combine. Refrigerate for at least 1 hour or overnight. To serve, put some ice into 4 to 6 glasses. Pour the tea over the ice. Tuck a sprig of mint into each glass and serve!

CHEF'S NOTE: *If you are gluten free, make certain to purchase certified gluten-free tea bags, available in most supermarkets.*

A tasty sauce, tangy dressing or savory spice blend all add flavor and punch to brighten up any plant-based meal. Here are some of my best flavor enhancers that will add jazzy-pizzazz to your dishes.

CHAPTER SIX

Dreamy Sauces AND DRESSINGS

Mushroom-Nut Burgers, *page 160*, with Quick Ketchup-Mayo Sauce, *page 87*

GLUTEN-FREE

This delectable substitute for the all-American classic can be used in place of dairy sour cream in any recipe that calls for sour cream.

JUST LIKE REAL Sour Cream

MAKES ABOUT 1⅓ CUPS

- ⅔ cup chopped raw cashews (see note)
- ½ cup water, plus more as needed
- 2 tablespoons freshly squeezed lemon juice
- ⅛ teaspoon of sea salt

Put the cashews, ½ cup water, lemon juice and sea salt into a blender and process until smooth and creamy, adding up to 2 additional tablespoons water if a thinner consistency is preferred. Stored tightly covered in the refrigerator, it will keep for up to 2 days.

CHEF'S NOTE: *For a creamier vegan sour cream, you may soak the cashews first. See instructions in the chef's note on page 83.*

GLUTEN-FREE

When you need a delicious mayonnaise, this simple recipe really fills the bill. I have served this to the fussiest of diners with great reviews!

VERY *Delicious* VEGAN MAYONNAISE

MAKES ABOUT 1¼ CUPS

- ¾ cup raw cashews (see note)
- ½ cup water, plus more as needed
- 1 tablespoon freshly squeezed lemon juice
- 2 teaspoons Dijon mustard
- 1 heaping teaspoon vegan cane sugar or your preferred dry sweetener

Put all of the ingredients in a blender and process until smooth, adding more water, 2 tablespoons at a time, to achieve the desired consistency. Refrigerate for 2 to 4 hours until chilled.

CHEF'S NOTE: *For a creamier mayo, you may soak the cashews first. Put the cashews and ½ cup water into a small bowl. Refrigerate for 1 to 4 hours. Drain the cashews and rinse thoroughly in cold water. Proceed with recipe as directed.*

Very Delicious Vegan Mayonnaise used in *All-American Potato Salad* (page 108).

GLUTEN-FREE

Marinating the tofu in this lively combination of Greek-style herbs and spices makes a delightful vegan "cheese." This recipe is updated with the yummy addition of mellow white miso paste, which kicks the flavor of the "feta" up a notch. Even if you're not a fan of tofu, you'll appreciate this tasty twist on a classic cheese.

Best VEGAN "FETA"

MAKES 4 SERVINGS

- **8 ounces firm or extra-firm regular tofu, well-drained and pressed** (see note about pressing tofu, page 220)
- **1½ tablespoons freshly squeezed lemon juice**
- **1 tablespoon plus 1 teaspoon extra-virgin olive oil**
- **1 heaping teaspoon gluten-free mellow white miso**
- **1 teaspoon Italian seasoning blend**
- **¼ teaspoon garlic powder**
- **¼ teaspoon sea salt, plus more to taste**

Put the tofu into a medium-sized bowl. Using your fingers or a fork, crumble the tofu until it resembles the texture of feta cheese (see note). Add the lemon juice, oil, miso, Italian seasoning, garlic powder and salt. Gently stir to combine. Cover and refrigerate for a minimum of 2 hours or up to 12 hours. Tightly covered and stored in the refrigerator, "feta" will keep for up to 3 days.

CHEF'S NOTE: *Alternately, you may cut the tofu into cubes for a "cubed" feta.*

GLUTEN-FREE

This easy-to-prepare, creamy cauliflower sauce stands in well whenever a "cream" sauce is called for. It's great served over steamed veggies or used in a casserole in place of the dairy version.

Cauliflower "CREAM" SAUCE

MAKES ABOUT 5 CUPS

- 4 cups bite-sized cauliflower florets
- ⅓ cup unsweetened nondairy milk, plus more as needed
- ⅓ cup vegetable broth
- 2 teaspoons extra-virgin olive oil
- 2 teaspoons gluten-free tamari
- ¼ teaspoon smoked paprika
- ¼ teaspoon ground turmeric (optional)
- ¼ teaspoon garlic powder
- ⅛ teaspoon sea salt, plus more to taste
- Freshly ground black (or white) pepper, to taste

Fit a steamer basket into a large pot with a tight-fitting lid. Add 2 to 3 inches of cold water, and then add the cauliflower. Cover, bring to a boil and steam about 7 minutes or until fork tender. Let cool 10 minutes.

Put the nondairy milk, broth, olive oil, tamari, paprika, optional turmeric, garlic powder, salt and several grinds of pepper in a blender container. Add the steamed cauliflower. Process until very smooth, adding a bit more nondairy milk, if needed, to achieve desired consistency. Season with more salt and pepper, to taste. The sauce is now ready to use in almost any recipe calling for cream sauce!

GLUTEN-FREE

This slightly spicy and sweet sauce makes the perfect flavored mayonnaise for a sandwich or burger, like *Powerhouse Burgers* (page 156) or *Crazy Easy BBQ Portobello Burgers* (page 167).

Creamy PAPRIKA SAUCE

MAKES ⅓ CUP

5 tablespoons vegan mayonnaise or *Very Delicious Vegan Mayonnaise* (page 83)

1 teaspoon maple syrup

¼ teaspoon smoked paprika

Sea salt, to taste

Freshly ground black pepper, to taste

Put all of the ingredients into a small bowl and whisk until thoroughly combined. Refrigerate the sauce until you are ready to use it. Stored tightly covered in the refrigerator, the sauce will keep for up to 3 days.

Creamy Paprika Sauce served on *Powerhouse Burgers* (page 156).

GLUTEN-FREE

This simple sauce dresses up vegan burgers, sandwiches or green salads.

QUICK *Ketchup-Mayo* SAUCE

MAKES ABOUT 3 TABLESPOONS

2 tablespoons vegan mayonnaise or *Very Delicious Vegan Mayonnaise* (page 83), **plus more to taste**

1 heaping tablespoon prepared ketchup, plus more to taste

Put all of the ingredients in a small bowl and briskly whisk to combine. Taste and add more ketchup or vegan mayonnaise, if desired.

VARIATION: *Quick Marinara-Mayo Sauce — Use 1 heaping tablespoon marinara sauce in place of the ketchup for a flavorful sauce with an Italian flair.*

VARIATION: *Pink Paprika Sauce—add ⅛ teaspoon smoked paprika and proceed as directed.*

Quick Marinara-Mayo Sauce served on *Sunny Black Bean Burgers* (page 162).

3 INGREDIENTS OR LESS

GLUTEN-FREE

This zingy sauce is based on my mom's tasty recipe. When served on the side, it can dress up many recipes like *Not So Crabby Cakes* (page 168) and *Quick Chickpea-Rice Burgers* (page 164).

CLASSIC *Cocktail* SAUCE

MAKES ABOUT ⅓ CUP

¼ cup ketchup

1½ tablespoons prepared horseradish, plus more as needed

1 teaspoon freshly squeezed lemon juice

Put all of the sauce ingredients in a small bowl. Stir to combine. Taste and add more horseradish, if desired. Cover and refrigerate until serving.

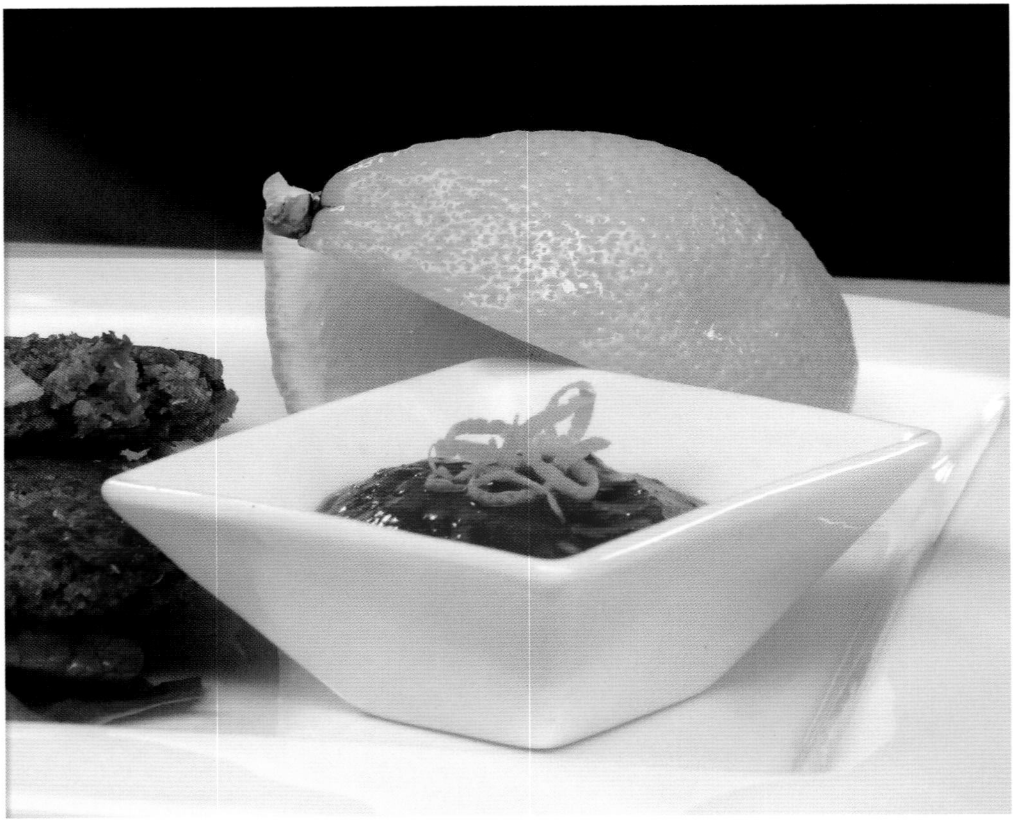

Three ingredients combined with fifteen minutes on the stovetop and you have a hearty and tasty sauce that's totally guest-worthy! Serve over your favorite whole-grain pasta and enjoy the compliments.

QUICKEST. Spaghetti Sauce. EVER.

MAKES 4 SERVINGS

1 package (8 ounces) **crumbled or ground seitan**

1 jar (24 to 28 ounces) **low-fat, vegan marinara sauce**

10 to 14 large fresh basil leaves, torn into pieces

Put the seitan and marinara sauce in a large skillet. Cover and bring to a simmer over medium heat. Decrease the heat to medium-low, cover and cook for 10 to 15 minutes, stirring occasionally, until heated through. Add the basil. Cover and cook 1 minute more.

Serve over spaghetti, capellini, penne or any other favorite style of pasta. You can also use this as a sauce in lasagna or a casserole.

JAZZY TIP: To make supper preparation easier, I keep store-bought, vegan marinara sauce and organic, BPA-free canned crushed and diced tomatoes in my pantry. Find several varieties that your family likes and keep them on hand for when you need to put together a tasty meal in a hurry.

This super yummy sauce will wake up just about any vegan burger, sandwich, veggie "steak" or kebab!

Out of This World PORTER BEER BBQ SAUCE

MAKES ABOUT 2 CUPS

- 1 cup ketchup
- 1 tablespoon gluten-free tamari
- 1 tablespoon extra-virgin olive oil
- 2 tablespoons unsulphured blackstrap molasses
- 1 tablespoon plus 2 teaspoons vegan dark brown sugar
- 1 teaspoon chili powder
- ¼ teaspoon garlic powder
- ⅛ teaspoon cayenne pepper
- ½ cup vegan porter or stout beer

Put all of the ingredients in a medium-sized saucepan. Bring to a simmer over medium-high heat. Decrease heat to medium-low and cook, stirring frequently, for 35 to 40 minutes or until the sauce has thickened and reduced by about one-third. The sauce is now ready to use.

This easy sauce delivers sweet *and* spicy flavors! It makes a snazzy option for adding tang and moisture to kebabs, veggie "steaks" or plant-based burgers, or anytime you need a quick, tasty barbecue sauce!

Easiest BBQ SAUCE

MAKES ABOUT ⅔ CUP

- ½ cup ketchup
- 2 tablespoons maple syrup
- 1½ teaspoons chili powder
- 1 teaspoon extra-virgin olive oil

Put all of the ingredients in a small bowl and briskly whisk to combine.

Easiest BBQ Sauce served on *Tasty Tofu-Veggie Kebabs* (page 227).

A cross between a light gravy and delicate sauce, this flavor-packed gravy highlights sweet onions and white button mushrooms, for an *almost* meaty taste.

Yummiest MUSHROOM-ONION GRAVY

MAKES ABOUT 3 CUPS

- **1 small sweet onion, thinly sliced**
- **1 tablespoon extra-virgin olive oil**
- **2 teaspoons gluten-free tamari**
- **12 ounces white button mushrooms, sliced**
- **2 teaspoons vegan buttery spread, divided**
- **2 tablespoons unbleached all-purpose flour, gluten-free flour or whole wheat flour** (see note)
- **2 cups water**
- **1 large vegan bouillon cube, crumbled** (see notes)

CHEF'S NOTE: *If preferred, you may use 2 cups of vegetable broth in place of the water and bouillon cube. Proceed with recipe as directed.*

Put the onion and olive oil into a large sauté pan and cook over medium heat for 3 minutes, stirring often. Add the tamari, cover and cook for 5 minutes or until the onion begins to soften and gets slightly brown around the edges. Add the mushrooms and 1 tablespoon of vegan buttery spread. Cover and cook for 3 minutes, stirring often.

Sprinkle the flour over the mushroom/onion mixture. Add the remaining tablespoon of vegan buttery spread. Cover and cook for 5 to 10 minutes, stirring often, until the flour is cooked and the mushrooms and onions become a dark caramel color. Add 2 cups of water and the crumbled bouillon cube and stir to combine.

Decrease the heat to medium-low, cover and let simmer, stirring occasionally, for 25 to 30 minutes or until the gravy begins to thicken *slightly* (the finished gravy has a thin consistency, see note). Serve hot over a meatless loaf, mashed potatoes, cooked grains, pasta or any recipe calling for a "beefy" tasting mushroom sauce!

CHEF'S NOTE: *For thicker gravy, after cooking for 25 minutes, reduce the heat to low and slowly simmer the gravy for up to 1 hour, stirring frequently, to allow it to further reduce.*

CHEF'S NOTE: *For a gluten-free option, use gluten-free flour (oat flour or a "1-to-1" style gluten-free flour work best) and a vegan, gluten-free bouillon cube in this recipe.*

Yummiest Mushroom-Onion Gravy served over *Nutty Zucchini Loaf* (page 216).

GLUTEN-FREE

This simple dressing is packed with flavor, making a welcome addition to any crisp, green salad.

LAURA'S FAVORITE *Balsamic* DRESSING

MAKES ABOUT ⅓ CUP

- 2 tablespoons extra-virgin olive oil
- 1½ tablespoons maple syrup
- 1 tablespoon Dijon or spicy brown mustard
- 1 tablespoon balsamic vinegar

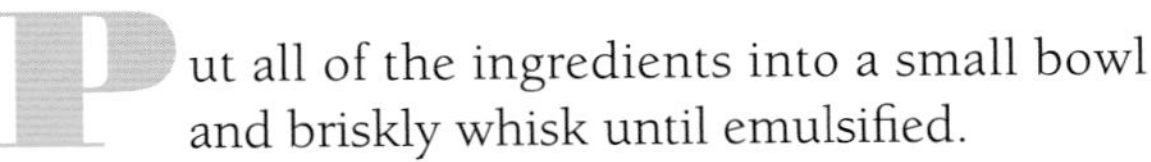

Put all of the ingredients into a small bowl and briskly whisk until emulsified.

GLUTEN-FREE

Let's all cheer for chickpeas! These yummy beans are often used in salads, stews, casseroles, soups and so much more. Here they take on a flavorsome twist to provide a tasty, creamy dressing to jazz up your leafy greens.

Hurray for Chickpeas DRESSING

MAKES 4 SERVINGS

- ¾ cup cooked chickpeas (garbanzo beans), drained and rinsed
- ½ cup water, plus more as needed
- 1 tablespoon freshly squeezed lemon juice
- 2 heaping teaspoons sesame tahini (purchase certified gluten-free tahini if you are gluten-free)
- 1 small clove garlic, peeled and chopped
- ½ teaspoon gluten-free tamari
- ⅛ teaspoon cayenne pepper
- ⅛ teaspoon sea salt, plus more as needed

Put all of the ingredients in a blender and process until smooth. If the dressing is too thick, add a small amount of water, 1 to 2 tablespoons at a time, to achieve the desired consistency. Taste and add more sea salt, if desired.

Laura's Favorite Balsamic Dressing served over *Delightful Dinner Salad* (page 116).

GLUTEN-FREE

This creamy sauce serves double duty as a salad dressing *and* a flavorful sauce. Serve it over a green salad, cooked grains or steamed veggies.

Tahini-Tamari DRESSING

MAKES 2 SERVINGS

2 tablespoons sesame tahini (purchase certified gluten-free tahini if you are gluten-free)

1 teaspoon gluten-free tamari, plus more as needed

1 to 2 tablespoons water, plus more as needed

Put the tahini, tamari and 1 tablespoon water in a small bowl. Whisk vigorously until creamy, adding more water to achieve desired consistency. (Use less water for a thicker consistency, more water for a thinner consistency.) Taste and add more tamari, if desired. Serve immediately.

Here's an economical way to have a quick Italian-style seasoning at your fingertips. Feel free to add your favorite dried herbs to create your own tasty blend. You can use this flavorsome blend anytime a recipe in this book calls for *Italian Seasoning Blend.*

LAURA'S Italian SEASONING BLEND

MAKES ABOUT 2½ TABLESPOONS

1 tablespoon dried basil

2½ teaspoons dried oregano

1½ teaspoons dried marjoram

½ teaspoon dried thyme

½ teaspoon dried rosemary

¼ teaspoon dried rubbed sage

Put all of the ingredients into a small bowl and stir to thoroughly combine. Stored in a tightly sealed container in a dry place away from sunlight, *Italian Seasoning Blend* will keep for 2 to 3 months.

GLUTEN-FREE

This cheese-less Parmesan incorporates tangy lemon zest to add zing, while the cashews provide a creamy texture and realistic taste.

CASHEW PARMESAN Cheeze

MAKES 8 SERVINGS

- ½ cup raw cashews
- ⅛ to ¼ teaspoon sea salt
- ½ teaspoon finely grated lemon zest

Put the cashews and salt in a blender and process until the consistency of crumbled Parmesan cheese. (Don't over process, or the cashews will turn into cashew butter!) Add the lemon zest and pulse several times to incorporate. Store tightly covered in the refrigerator for up to 3 days.

This spice combination is one of my mom's wonderful recipes. It showcases the perfect blend of flavors to enhance any pumpkin pie, cookie or cake that calls for this classic sweet-and-spicy blend.

Mom's PUMPKIN PIE SPICE

MAKES ¼ CUP

- 1 tablespoon ground cinnamon
- 1 tablespoon ground ginger
- 1 tablespoon ground nutmeg
- 1 tablespoon ground allspice

Put all of the ingredients in a small bowl and stir with a dry whisk to combine. Stored in a tightly sealed container in a dry place away from sunlight, *Pumpkin Pie Spice* will keep for 2 to 3 months.

Whether first course or main course, based in greens, nuts, seeds or grains or tossed with a sweet or savory dressing, a colorful salad always makes a meal shine. In this chapter I share some of my favorite combinations for serving up crunchy raw veggies and crisp leafy greens!

CHAPTER
SEVEN
Raw-Some Plates

All-American Potato Salad, *page 108*

GLUTEN-FREE OPTION

With a tasty and tangy dressing, tender tiny potatoes, colorful green beans, savory baked tofu, creamy chickpeas, fresh tomatoes and salty olives, this satisfying dish is reminiscent of the French classic. Hearty and filling, it's the perfect salad to serve for a supper entrée or as a first course for a fancy soirée.

JAZZY Salad Niçoise with Lemon-Dijon Dressing

MAKES 2 TO 3 (LARGE, MAIN DISH) SERVINGS OR 6 TO 8 (FIRST COURSE) SERVINGS

LEMON-DIJON DRESSING (SEE NOTE)

2 tablespoons extra-virgin olive oil, plus more to taste

2 tablespoons freshly squeezed lemon juice

1½ tablespoons maple syrup

1½ heaping tablespoons Dijon or spicy brown mustard

¼ teaspoon garlic powder

¼ teaspoon sea salt

Freshly ground black pepper, to taste

1 heaping tablespoon thinly sliced scallions (white *and* light green parts), **plus more for garnish**

CHEF'S NOTE: *If you like a lot of dressing on your salad, prepare a double batch of the dressing and use more dressing on each salad. This yummy dressing is delicious on any green salad!*

To make the dressing, put all of the dressing ingredients into a small bowl and briskly whisk until well combined. Taste and add 1 more tablespoon olive oil, if desired

To make the salad, fit a steamer basket into a large pot with a tight-fitting lid. Add 2 to 3 inches of cold water. Add the potatoes. Cover, bring to a boil and steam 18 to 20 minutes or until fork tender. Transfer the potatoes to a medium-sized bowl and let cool 15 minutes. Toss the potatoes with a scant 2 tablespoons of the dressing, cover and refrigerate until you are ready to assemble the salad.

Fit the same steamer basket back into the pot. Add 2 to 3 inches of cold water. Add the green beans. Cover, bring to a boil and steam 5 to 8 minutes or until crisp tender. Transfer the beans to a medium-sized bowl and let cool 15 minutes. Toss the beans with a scant 2 tablespoons of the dressing, cover and refrigerate until you are ready to assemble the salad.

SALAD

2½ cups baby red and/or white potatoes, cut in half

2½ to 3 cups green beans, trimmed and left whole

10 to 12 romaine lettuce leaves

3 Campari tomatoes, quartered or 12 cherry tomatoes, cut in half

8 ounces cold *Maple Baked Tofu* (page 220) or store-bought baked tofu, cubed (see note)

1 cup cooked chickpeas (garbanzo beans, see note)

4 to 6 large radishes, sliced

6 to 9 queen green olives, with pimento

8 to 12 pitted Kalamata olives

Sea salt, to taste

Several grinds freshly ground black pepper, to taste

To assemble the salad for a main dish entrée, put 3 large romaine lettuce leaves on each of two to three large dinner plates (see note). Arrange the potatoes and green beans in separate rows on the plate. Add the tomatoes, cubed tofu, chickpeas, radish slices, queen green olives and Kalamata olives, all arranged in separate rows on the plate (see photo). At this point the salads may be covered and refrigerated for up to 2 hours. Right before serving, drizzle about 1½ tablespoons of dressing over each of the salads. Top with sea salt and freshly ground black pepper, to taste, and serve.

CHEF'S NOTE: *For a gluten-free and soy-free option, substitute an additional 1 cup of the cooked chickpeas in place of the baked tofu.*

CHEF'S NOTE: *To serve this salad as a first course or side dish, divide and arrange the ingredients on six to eight pretty salad plates.*

A quick and tasty salad can be on the table in less than 20 minutes with this delightful recipe featuring cooked, whole wheat couscous. If you would like to make this dish gluten-free, simply substitute cooked quinoa or brown rice for the couscous.

Couscous, WALNUT AND TOMATO SALAD

MAKES 4 TO 6 SERVINGS

SALAD

3½ cups *cooked* and cooled whole wheat couscous, brown rice or quinoa (see note)

1 teaspoon all-purpose seasoning

½ teaspoon dried parsley

16 to 18 grape or cherry tomatoes, halved

½ cup chopped walnuts

1 large stalk of celery, with leaves, diced

18 to 20 pitted Kalamata olives, diced

¼ teaspoon sea salt, plus more to taste

DRESSING

2 tablespoons freshly squeezed lemon juice

1½ tablespoons extra-virgin olive oil, plus more as needed

Dash of garlic powder

Dash of cayenne pepper

Several grinds freshly ground black pepper

To make the salad, put the cooked couscous, all-purpose seasoning, parsley, tomatoes, walnuts, celery and olives in a large bowl and stir to combine. Sprinkle with sea salt and stir to combine.

To make the dressing, put the lemon juice, olive oil, garlic powder and cayenne pepper in a small bowl and briskly whisk to combine. Pour the dressing over the salad and gently stir to combine. Add black pepper and more salt to taste. Cover and refrigerate for 1 to 6 hours before serving.

CHEF'S NOTE: *To make this recipe gluten-free, be sure to use cooked brown rice or quinoa in place of the couscous.*

GLUTEN-FREE

I first served this to guests for a casual lunch. I wanted something light, but I wanted it to be attractive and impressive. Packed with fresh summer produce and plenty of plant-powered protein, this salad makes a lovely luncheon entrée or nice supper side.

COLORFUL *Quinoa* SALAD

MAKES 6 TO 8 SERVINGS

SALAD

1½ cups *uncooked* quinoa, thoroughly rinsed and drained

3 cups water

1 vegan bouillon cube, crumbled (see note)

1½ cups chopped tomatoes

¾ cup finely chopped baby spinach

½ cup finely chopped sweet onion

¼ cup peeled, seeded and diced cucumber

DRESSING

3 tablespoons freshly squeezed lemon juice

2 tablespoons extra-virgin olive oil, plus more to taste

1 teaspoon maple syrup

1 tablespoon freshly chopped flat-leaf parsley, plus several sprigs for garnish

¼ teaspoon garlic powder or 1 small clove of garlic, finely minced

Put the quinoa, water and bouillon cube in a medium-sized saucepan. Cover and bring to a boil over medium-high heat. Decrease the heat to medium-low and simmer for 15 to 17 minutes or until all of the water is absorbed and the quinoa is soft. Let cool for 30 minutes. Cover tightly and refrigerate for 2 hours or overnight. Several hours before serving the salad, put the cold quinoa, tomatoes, spinach, onion and cucumber in a large bowl and gently stir, using a large spoon, to combine.

To make the dressing, put the lemon juice, olive oil, maple syrup, parsley and garlic powder in a small bowl and briskly whisk to emulsify. Pour the dressing over the salad and gently stir until combined. Taste and add more olive oil, if desired. Cover and refrigerate for 1 to 4 hours, so the flavors marry. Serve cold (see serving suggestion).

CHEF'S NOTE: *If you are gluten free, use a certified gluten-free* and *vegan bouillon cube in this recipe.*

SERVING SUGGESTION: *If you would like to present individual servings of this salad in an elegant manner, put a 3-inch ring mold in the center of each salad-sized plate (pictured on opposite page). Fill the mold to the top with quinoa salad and press down with a spoon (or mold press) to pack the salad tightly into the mold. Carefully remove the mold. Repeat with the remaining salads and serve.*

GLUTEN-FREE

Lentils provide a substantial base and plenty of plant-based protein, while the veggies and flavorings add zing to this satisfying salad.

French LENTIL SALAD BOWL with Sweet Peppers and Basil

MAKES 4 SERVINGS

- 4 cups *cooked* French green lentils, well chilled (see note)
- ⅔ cup diced sweet onion
- 1 medium red sweet bell pepper, seeded and chopped
- 1 large avocado, peeled, pitted and chopped
- ½ cup chopped fresh basil
- 2 tablespoons extra-virgin olive oil
- 2 tablespoons freshly squeezed lemon juice
- 1 heaping teaspoon chili powder
- ½ teaspoon sea salt

Put all of the ingredients into a large bowl and gently stir to combine. Spoon into deep bowls and serve at room temperature, or cover and refrigerate for up to 2 hours and serve cold.

CHEF'S NOTE: *Lentils don't need to be presoaked, but check for small stones and rinse them well before preparing. To cook lentils, put 4 cups water and 2 cups dry lentils into a large saucepan and bring to a boil over medium-high heat. Decrease the heat to low, cover and cook for 35 to 40 minutes, stirring occasionally. Add more water if the pan becomes dry. The lentils are done when they are soft (they do not need to absorb all of the water). Drain off any excess water in a fine-meshed strainer. Yields 4 to 5 cups cooked lentils.*

French Lentil Salad Bowl *(page 106), above*

All-American Potato Salad *(page 108), below*

GLUTEN-FREE

This hearty summertime salad is one of my favorite vegan versions of the classic American staple. It's a genuine crowd pleaser and will brighten up any warm weather meal.

All-American POTATO SALAD

MAKES 8 SERVINGS

SALAD

4 pounds red or white potatoes, peeled and cubed (see note)

2 large carrots, peeled and thinly sliced (see note)

2 large stalks of celery with leaves, thinly sliced

1 large red sweet bell pepper, seeded and chopped

10 large green queen olives, with pimentos, diced

½ cup chopped fresh parsley

½ cup chopped fresh basil

DRESSING

1 cup vegan mayonnaise or *Very Delicious Vegan Mayonnaise* (page 83)

¼ cup spicy brown or Dijon mustard

2 tablespoons maple syrup

2 teaspoons Italian seasoning blend

½ teaspoon sea salt

Freshly ground black pepper, to taste

Fit a steamer basket into a large pot with a tight-fitting lid. Add 2 to 3 inches of cold water, and then add the potatoes. Cover, bring to a boil and steam 18 to 22 minutes or until fork tender. Spread the potato cubes in a single layer on a large, rimmed baking sheet and allow to cool for 15 minutes. Cover and refrigerate the potatoes for at least 30 minutes or up to 24 hours before assembling the salad.

Put the chilled potatoes, carrots, celery, red pepper and olives into a large bowl and stir with a large spoon to combine.

To make the dressing, put the vegan mayonnaise, mustard, maple syrup, Italian seasoning, sea salt and several grinds of black pepper into a small bowl and stir to combine. Add the dressing to the potato mixture and fold it into the salad to coat. Add the parsley and basil and gently fold it into the potato salad. Cover and refrigerate for at least 3 hours, or up to 8 hours before serving. The dressing will be absorbed into the potatoes as the salad chills, so if it seems dry, add more vegan mayonnaise and/or mustard right before serving, to taste.

CHEF'S NOTE: *If preferred, you may leave the peels on the potatoes and the carrots, but the texture of the salad will become denser.*

See photo of this recipe on page 107.

GLUTEN-FREE

A simple salad that packs a punch of flavor and crunch, this dish makes the perfect accompaniment to a company meal or weeknight family supper.

ROMAINE, SWEET PEPPER AND WALNUT *Salad*

MAKES 6 SERVINGS

SALAD

1 medium head romaine lettuce, torn into bite-sized pieces

6 to 8 mini sweet peppers, seeded and thinly sliced

⅓ cup chopped walnuts

DRESSING

2 tablespoons extra-virgin olive oil

2 tablespoons balsamic vinegar

1 tablespoon maple syrup

1 teaspoon Dijon or spicy brown mustard

Put all of the salad ingredients into a large bowl. Put the dressing ingredients into a small bowl and whisk to emulsify. Pour the dressing over the salad. Toss and serve!

CHEF'S NOTE: *If desired, top the salad with shredded vegan parmesan cheese for extra pizzazz!*

This spud salad has a little something extra. The addition of chickpeas adds a delightful pop of protein, while still imparting the hearty satisfaction you get from traditional potato salad. Crisp celery and carrots, along with tangy olives, round out this tasty summertime staple.

SALAD

MAKES 8 SERVINGS

SALAD

2 pounds baby Dutch yellow potatoes, or your preferred baby potato variety, cut in half if large

1 can (14 to 16 ounces) chickpeas (garbanzo beans), drained and rinsed

10 Queen green olives, with pimento, diced

2 to 3 ribs of celery, diced

1 very large carrot, diced (peeling is optional)

1 tablespoon minced celery leaves

Freshly ground black pepper, to taste

DRESSING

6 tablespoons vegan mayonnaise or *Very Delicious Vegan Mayonnaise* (page 83)

3 tablespoons spicy brown mustard or Dijon mustard

1 tablespoon maple syrup

1 teaspoon Italian seasoning blend

½ teaspoon sea salt

Scant ⅛ teaspoon cayenne pepper (optional)

GARNISH

Freshly ground black pepper, to taste

Smoked paprika, to taste

Several sprigs fresh parsley or small kale leaves

Fit a steamer basket into a large pot with a tight-fitting lid. Add 2 to 3 inches of cold water, and then add the baby potatoes. Steam the potatoes for 16 to 20 minutes or until they are fork tender. Spread the potatoes in a single layer on a large, rimmed baking sheet and allow to cool for 15 minutes. Cover and refrigerate the potatoes for at least 30 minutes or up to 24 hours before assembling the salad. To assemble the salad, put the potatoes, chickpeas, olives, celery, carrots and minced celery leaves into a large bowl and stir with a large spoon to combine.

To make the dressing, put the vegan mayonnaise, mustard, maple syrup, Italian seasoning, salt and optional cayenne pepper in a small bowl and briskly whisk to combine. Pour the dressing over the potato mixture and stir to combine. Add several grinds of black pepper, to taste, and stir to combine. Transfer the salad to a pretty serving bowl and sprinkle with smoked paprika. Top with parsley sprigs or kale leaves. Cover with plastic wrap and refrigerate for 2 to 4 hours before serving.

Perfect to serve for a warm-weather entrée, this herbed pasta salad gets a nice pop of protein from the black beans, while the peppers add color and crunch. Zingy marinated artichokes add a jazzy twist to this family friendly staple.

BLACK BEAN AND ARTICHOKE *Pasta Salad* with Fresh Herbs

MAKES 8 TO 10 SERVINGS

SALAD

1 pound cooked and cooled small pasta shells (see note)

1 can (15 to 16 ounces) black beans, drained and rinsed

5 carrots, cut in julienne strips or grated (peeling is optional)

2 red and/or orange sweet bell peppers, seeded and chopped

½ small sweet onion, diced

1 jar (8 to 12 ounces) marinated artichoke hearts, drained and chopped

12 to 14 large leaves chopped fresh basil, plus sprigs for garnish

4 leaves minced fresh oregano

1 to 2 leaves minced fresh sage

2 heaping tablespoons chopped fresh parsley

DRESSING

⅓ cup vegan mayonnaise or *Very Delicious Vegan Mayonnaise* (page 83), plus more as needed

¼ cup Dijon or spicy brown mustard, plus more as needed

1 tablespoon vegan brown or cane sugar (optional)

1 teaspoon Italian seasoning blend

½ teaspoon sea salt, plus more to taste

¼ teaspoon ground turmeric

Several grinds freshly ground black pepper

Put all of the salad ingredients into a very large bowl. Put all of the dressing ingredients in a small bowl and briskly whisk until smooth. Add the dressing to the salad and toss gently until well combined. If the salad still seems a bit dry, add more vegan mayonnaise and/or mustard to achieve desired consistency. Season with additional salt and pepper, to taste. Cover and refrigerate for 2 to 4 hours or until the salad is thoroughly chilled. Serve over a bed of crisp greens, garnished with a sprig of fresh basil.

CHEF'S NOTE: *If desired, you may use penne or fusilli pasta in place of the small pasta shells in this recipe.*

Photo courtesy of Annie Olivero. Learn more about Annie on page 296.

GLUTEN-FREE

I like to serve a green salad with nuts and dried cranberries during the winter holidays. This festive salad celebrates the season with healthy ingredients, vibrant colors, tantalizing textures and delicious flavors!

Baby Greens, CARROT AND CRANBERRY SALAD

MAKES 4 TO 6 SERVINGS

SALAD

6 cups lightly packed baby greens

1 cup grated carrots (peeling is optional)

⅓ cup sweetened dried cranberries

½ cup chopped pecans

DRESSING

3 tablespoons freshly squeezed lemon juice

2 tablespoons extra-virgin olive oil

2 tablespoons maple syrup

⅛ teaspoon sea salt

Several grinds black pepper

Put all of the salad ingredients into a large bowl. Put all of the dressing ingredients into a small bowl and briskly whisk to combine. Pour the dressing over the salad and gently toss to coat. Serve immediately, or cover and refrigerate for up to 30 minutes before serving.

GLUTEN-FREE

Fresh and fabulous, this quick salad combines refreshing cucumbers, tiny tomatoes and sweet pepper rings drizzled in a very light balsamic dressing that lets the taste of the veggies shine through.

CUCUMBER, TOMATO AND MINI-PEPPER *Salad*

MAKES 4 TO 6 SERVINGS

SALAD

- 1⅔ cups sliced cucumber (peeling is optional)
- ¾ cup bite-sized grape tomatoes
- ¾ cup seeded and sliced orange and/or red mini sweet peppers
- 2 heaping tablespoons chopped fresh parsley
- 1 heaping tablespoon thinly sliced fresh basil

DRESSING

- 1 tablespoon extra-virgin olive oil, plus more to taste
- ½ tablespoon balsamic vinegar, plus more to taste
- ⅛ to ¼ teaspoon sea salt
- Freshly ground black pepper, to taste

Put the cucumber, tomatoes and mini pepper slices into a medium-sized bowl and gently toss to combine. Put all of the dressing ingredients into a small bowl and briskly whisk to emulsify. Taste and add a bit more olive oil and/or vinegar, if desired. Pour the dressing over the cucumber mixture and stir to coat. Add the parsley and basil and gently toss to combine. Let stand 5 to 15 minutes and serve.

This straightforward but flavorful salad is an excellent choice to serve as a first course at a casual gathering or family meal.

Delightful DINNER SALAD

MAKES 4 SERVINGS

5 ounces baby spring greens or your preferred mix of greens

¼ small sweet onion, thinly sliced

4 Campari tomatoes (cut into quarters) or 12 whole grape tomatoes

3 large radishes, thinly sliced

1 medium carrot, cut in julienne strips (peeling is optional)

4 to 6 tablespoons *Laura's Favorite Balsamic Salad Dressing* (page 94)

Sea salt, to taste

Freshly ground black pepper, to taste

Put one-quarter of the baby spring greens into each of four salad bowls. Arrange 4 tomato quarters (or 4 grape tomatoes) around the perimeter of each bowl. Scatter one-quarter of the radish slices and one-quarter of the onion slices over the greens. Put the carrots in a little mound over the top of the greens, in the center of the salad. Drizzle each salad with 1 to 1½ tablespoons of dressing. Add sea salt and black pepper, if desired and serve.

GLUTEN-FREE

Apples add a tart and sweet taste to delicate baby spinach in this appetizing salad. Raisins and pumpkin seeds provide texture and flavor, while the dressing adds real zing!

SPINACH AND APPLE *Salad* with Maple-Mustard Dressing

MAKES 4 TO 6 SERVINGS

SALAD

8 cups lightly packed baby spinach

1 large apple, peeled and thinly sliced

3 tablespoons raisins

2 tablespoons pumpkin seeds (raw or roasted)

Sea salt, to taste

Freshly ground black pepper, to taste

DRESSING

3 tablespoons maple syrup

3 tablespoons Dijon mustard

1 small clove garlic, finely minced

¼ teaspoon sea salt

Dash cayenne

CHEF'S NOTE: *The dressing may make more than you'll use for this salad, but it's a great basic dressing to have on hand. Stored in an airtight container in the refrigerator, leftover dressing will keep for about 3 days.*

Put the spinach, apple slices, raisins and pumpkin seeds in a large bowl. To make the dressing, put the maple syrup, mustard, garlic, ¼ teaspoon sea salt and cayenne in a small bowl and briskly whisk until smooth. Pour 4 tablespoons of the dressing over the salad and toss gently to coat the spinach leaves. Taste and add more dressing, if desired, plus salt and pepper, to taste.

This recipe is from *Laura Theodore's Jazzy Vegetarian Classics: Vegan Twists on American Family Favorites* (BenBella Books, 2013). Reprinted with permission. Learn more at www.benbellabooks.com.

3 INGREDIENTS OR LESS

GLUTEN-FREE

Easy, tasty and nutritious, this unique dish is lovely too! Avocados provide an edible bowl, while crunchy walnuts and tangy dried berries impart a satisfying stuffing.

AVOCADO *Boats* WITH WALNUTS AND CRANBERRIES

MAKES 4 SERVINGS

⅓ cup chopped walnuts

⅓ cup sweetened dried cranberries, raisins or dried cherries

2 medium avocados, halved and pitted (leave peels on)

Put the walnuts and cranberries into a small bowl and toss to combine. Fill each avocado half with the walnut/cranberry mixture, mounding it slightly. Place on an attractive salad plate and serve.

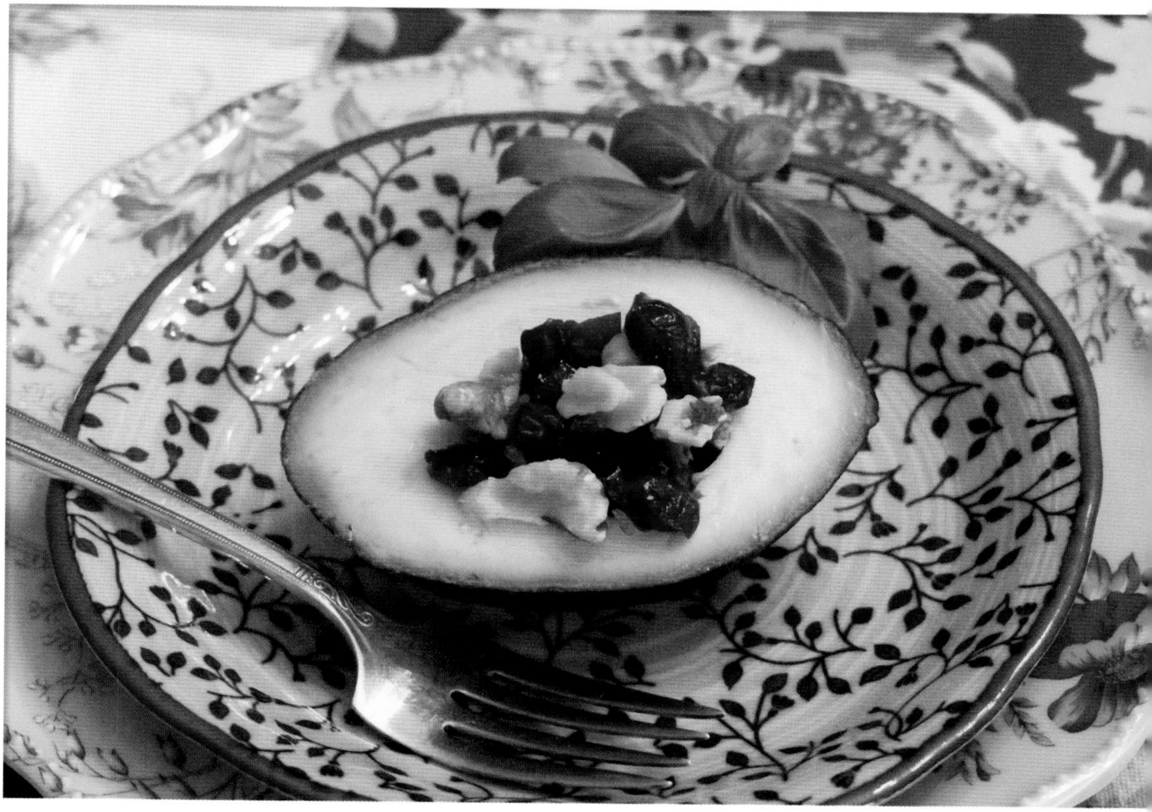

Hot soups stand front and center as a main dish in colder seasons, while chilled soups are perfect to serve for refreshing summer fare. No matter what the season, a satisfying potage makes a family-friendly addition to your weekly menu plan.

CHAPTER

EIGHT

Time for Soup

Red Lentil-Potato Curry Soup, *page 132*

GLUTEN-FREE

This refreshing, fruity soup is truly an eye-catching, tasty experience. A rich lemony cashew cream is swirled into fresh blueberry purée to make an inviting first course offering.

COLD *Blueberry* SOUP with Lemon-Cashew Cream

MAKES 4 TO 5 SERVINGS

LEMON-CASHEW CREAM

⅓ cup plus 2 tablespoons raw cashews

1 cup water, divided

2 tablespoons maple syrup

1½ tablespoons freshly squeezed lemon juice

BLUEBERRY SOUP

2½ cups fresh blueberries, plus 12 to 15 more for garnish

1 cup unsweetened nondairy milk

2 tablespoons maple syrup

To make the cream, put the cashews and ½ cup water into the refrigerator and let soak for 1 to 4 hours. Drain the cashews and rinse thoroughly in cold water. Put the soaked cashews, ½ cup water, maple syrup and lemon juice into a blender and process until very smooth. Transfer to a covered container and refrigerate for 3 to 4 hours, until completely cold.

To make the soup, put the blueberries, nondairy milk and maple syrup into a blender and process until smooth. Transfer to a covered container and refrigerate for 3 to 4 hours, until completely cold. The soup may separate while it chills, so stir the blueberry soup thoroughly before serving, making certain it becomes a smooth purée again.

To serve, divide the blueberry soup into 4 to 5 small bowls. Swirl some of the cashew cream on top of each soup and garnish with three fresh blueberries. Put the remaining cashew cream in a small pitcher to pass around the table so that diners can add more "cream" to their soup, if desired (see note).

> **CHEF'S NOTE**: *Tightly covered and refrigerated, leftover* Lemon-Cashew Cream *will keep for 2 days.*

GLUTEN-FREE

The creamy texture of the avocados in this summer soup is enhanced by soft tofu, which, along with the avocados, stands in for the heavy cream so often used in cold soups. It's a refreshing starter when the temperature is on the rise!

Avocado-LEMON SOUP

MAKES 4 TO 8 SERVINGS

2 small avocados, halved, pitted, peeled and chopped

⅔ block (about 12 ounces) soft silken or soft regular tofu, drained and cubed

2 tablespoons minced sweet onion

2 tablespoons freshly squeezed lemon juice, plus more to taste

½ small clove garlic, minced (optional)

1 teaspoon vegan cane sugar or maple syrup

½ teaspoon chopped fresh parsley

¼ teaspoon sea salt, plus more to taste

⅛ teaspoon cayenne pepper

¼ cup water, plus more as needed

Several grinds freshly ground black pepper, to taste

Minced red sweet bell peppers, for garnish

Put the chopped avocados, tofu, onion, lemon juice, garlic, sugar, parsley, salt, cayenne pepper and water in a blender and process until creamy. Add more water, 2 tablespoons at a time, to achieve the desired consistency. Transfer to a bowl, taste and season with black pepper and additional salt, if desired. Cover and refrigerate for 4 hours, or until cold. Ladle the soup into espresso cups or small soup bowls. Garnish with sweet peppers and serve.

Velvety Carrot Soup *(page 127)*, *above*

Cool Cucumber Soup *(page 129)*, *below*

GLUTEN-FREE

This creamy chilled soup is a wonderful first course for a festive, summertime meal. The refreshing taste of the cucumber is carried by the tofu, which adds substance and stands in for the heavy cream so often called for in similar soups. Whenever I serve this dish, it's always a *big* hit and diners inevitably ask, "Are you *sure* there isn't any cream in this soup?"

Cool CUCUMBER SOUP

MAKES 4 SERVINGS

- 2 medium cucumbers, peeled, seeded and chopped
- 12 ounces soft or firm regular tofu, drained and cubed
- ½ sweet onion, chopped
- 2 tablespoons freshly squeezed lemon juice
- 1 small clove garlic, chopped
- 1 teaspoon vegan brown sugar
- 1 tablespoon finely chopped fresh dill or 1 teaspoon dried dill weed
- Sea salt, to taste
- Freshly ground black pepper, to taste
- 4 dill or parsley sprigs, for garnish (optional)

Put the chopped cucumbers, tofu, onion, lemon juice, garlic, brown sugar and one-quarter of the dill in a blender and process until creamy. Transfer to a bowl and stir in the remaining dill. Season with salt and pepper, to taste. Cover and refrigerate for 4 to 6 hours. About 30 minutes before serving, chill four soup bowls. To serve, ladle the soup into the chilled bowls. Garnish each bowl with a dill or parsley sprig. Serve immediately. It's dill-icious!

GLUTEN-FREE

I love a root vegetable-based soup, and this one is enhanced with canned tomatoes and sweet onions, along with a few other snazzy vegetables. It makes an excellent cold weather potage.

Tasty TOMATO AND ROOT VEGGIE SOUP

MAKES 4 TO 5 SERVINGS

5 medium red potatoes, sliced (peeling is optional)

4 large carrots, sliced (peeling is optional)

1 very large sweet potato, peeled and cubed

1 small sweet onion, sliced

1 can (24 to 28 ounces) **crushed tomatoes**

5 cups water, plus more as needed

1 tablespoon extra-virgin olive oil

1 teaspoon Italian seasoning blend

1 teaspoon gluten-free tamari

1 large vegan bouillon cube, crumbled (see note)

1½ cups green beans, trimmed and cut in 1½ -inch pieces

Put the red potatoes, carrots, sweet potato and onion into a large soup pot. Add the crushed tomatoes and the water and stir to combine. Add the olive oil, Italian seasoning, tamari and bouillon cube. Cover and bring to a boil over medium-high heat. Decrease the heat to medium-low, cover and simmer for 25 minutes, stirring occasionally. If the soup becomes too thick, add a bit more water, as needed. Stir in the green beans, cover and simmer, stirring occasionally, for 30 minutes or until all of the vegetables are tender. Ladle into soup bowls and serve.

JAZZY TIP: If you are cooking gluten-free, make certain to use a vegan, gluten-free bouillon cube in this recipe.

GLUTEN-FREE

Rich and creamy tasting, this hearty, low-fat soup makes ideal fall fare for a nutritious supper entrée or first course offering. This recipe makes great use of leftover cooked quinoa!

BUTTERNUT SQUASH AND QUINOA *Bisque*

MAKES 3 TO 4 SERVINGS

1½ cups peeled, seeded and cubed butternut squash

1 cup *cooked* quinoa

1½ cups unsweetened nondairy milk, plus more as needed

½ cup orange juice, plus more as needed

1 heaping teaspoon vegan brown sugar

¼ teaspoon ground cumin

¼ teaspoon gluten-free tamari

⅛ teaspoon sea salt, plus more as needed

Freshly ground black pepper, to taste

3 to 4 sprigs of fresh parsley or sage, for garnish

Fit a steamer basket into a large pot with a tight-fitting lid. Add 2 to 3 inches of cold water, and then add the butternut squash. Cover, bring to a boil and steam 20 to 25 minutes or until fork tender. Transfer the butternut squash to a bowl and let cool 15 minutes. Put the squash, cooked quinoa, nondairy milk, orange juice, brown sugar, cumin, tamari and sea salt in a blender. Process until smooth. If the mixture seems too thick, add more nondairy milk or orange juice to achieve the desired consistency.

Pour the butternut squash mixture into a soup pot. Bring the soup to a simmer and cook over medium-low heat for about 10 minutes, stirring often, until heated through, adding more nondairy milk if the soup begins to thicken too much. Season with salt and black pepper, to taste. To serve, ladle into soup bowls and garnish with a sprig of parsley or sage.

GLUTEN-FREE

Needing only fifteen minutes to prep and seven ingredients to assemble, this soup is an excellent candidate for a nutritious lunch or informal supper. As the red lentils cook, they break down to magically thicken the broth. Before you know it, you have a hearty, delicious soup, ready to serve.

RED LENTIL-POTATO *Curry* SOUP

MAKES 4 SERVINGS

32 ounces vegetable broth

2 cups peeled and diced red or white potatoes

1½ cups sliced carrots (peeling is optional)

1 cup *uncooked* red lentils, sorted and thoroughly rinsed (see note)

8 ounces cremini or white button mushrooms, diced

½ cup water, plus more as needed

½ teaspoon curry powder (see note)

Sea salt, to taste (optional)

Put all of the ingredients in a medium-sized soup pot and bring to a boil over medium-high heat. Once boiling, decrease the heat to medium-low, cover and simmer 45 to 50 minutes, stirring occasionally, until the vegetables are tender and the lentils are soft. Taste and add sea salt, if desired. Serve piping hot.

CHEF'S NOTE: *To sort the lentils, spread them out in a single layer on a large baking sheet. Remove any stones, dirt, broken lentils or other debris. The lentils are now ready to be rinsed and used in your recipe. You may also sort split peas or dried beans in this manner.*

CHEF'S NOTE: *For a more pronounced curry flavor, you may use up to 1 rounded teaspoon curry powder in this recipe.*

One day, I had some baby bok choy in my refrigerator and decided to whip up a quick miso-*style* soup. The result is a simple but totally tasty soup that takes just 25 minutes to prepare.

BABY BOK CHOY-*Miso* SOUP

MAKES 3 TO 4 SERVINGS

- 1 cup thinly sliced carrots (peeling is optional)
- ½ cup seeded and thinly sliced red sweet bell pepper
- 32 ounces vegetable broth
- 1 medium bunch baby bok choy with leaves, bottom trimmed off and thinly sliced
- 1 heaping teaspoon gluten-free mellow white miso
- 2 tablespoons thinly sliced scallions, white and green parts

Put the sliced carrots, peppers and vegetable broth into a medium-sized saucepan. Cover and bring to a boil over medium heat. Decrease the heat to medium-low and cook for 4 minutes, stirring occasionally. Add the baby bok choy and cook for 4 minutes or until the carrots, pepper and bok choy are tender. Decrease the heat to low. Ladle out 3 to 4 tablespoons of the broth and pour it into a soup bowl. Stir the miso into the hot broth, briskly whisking until smooth. Add the miso mixture back into the soup pot. Add the scallions to the soup and gently cook for about 2 minutes, taking care not to bring the soup to a boil (see note). Serve as a first course or light luncheon entrée.

CHEF'S NOTE: *Since miso is a fermented food (meaning it contains live, active cultures of "good" bacteria), be careful not to vigorously boil it. Doing so diminishes the probiotics in the miso, nixing the health benefits it offers, like better digestive health.*

Of course, sandwiches make classic luncheon fare, but I say, "Why not think *outside* the lunch box?" Vegan sandwiches are fit for any meal of the day! From *Rockin' Peanut-Butter and Banana Toast* for breakfast to *Italian "Sausage" and Pepper Hoagies* for a fun family supper to *Cucumber Tea Sandwiches with Basil-Chili "Butter"* for an afternoon tea, this chapter is filled with savory sandwiches and spreads that everyone will love!

CHAPTER NINE

Yummy Sandwiches AND SPREADS

Pretty Paprika-Chickpea Finger Sandwiches, *page 139*

GLUTEN-FREE OPTION

These delicate sandwiches make a bold statement with crisp cucumbers and a slightly spicy, pink-hued buttery spread. They are so pretty to serve, too!

CUCUMBER *Tea Sandwiches* with Basil-Chili "Butter"

MAKES ABOUT 15 PETITE SANDWICHES

BASIL-CHILI "BUTTER"

⅓ cup vegan buttery spread, softened

6 to 8 large leaves minced fresh basil

¼ teaspoon chili powder

Scant ¼ teaspoon sea salt

SANDWICHES

½ small English (seedless) **cucumber, partially peeled** (see note)

10 medium slices vegan whole-grain "white-style" bread (or vegan *and* gluten-free bread for a gluten-free option)

GARNISH

15 small basil leaves

15 toothpicks

CHEF'S NOTE: *The* Basil-Chili "Butter" *is wonderful to serve on freshly cooked corn-on-the-cob or to spread on crusty whole-grain bread, corn bread or warm muffins!*

Put all of the *Basil-Chili "Butter"* ingredients into a small bowl and vigorously stir with a fork until well combined. Cut the cucumber into thin slices using a sharp knife. Using a 2-inch cookie cutter, cut 3 circles out of each slice of bread (see note) to make 30 rounds.

Line a medium-sized rimmed baking pan with unbleached parchment paper. To assemble your sandwiches, spread some of the *Basil-Chili "Butter"* on one side of each of the 30 bread rounds. Put a round on the parchment, top it with 1 or 2 cucumber slices, and then top with another bread round. Garnish with a basil leaf secured with a toothpick. Repeat with the remaining rounds and cucumber slices. Arrange on a nice platter or cake stand. Cover tightly and refrigerate for 15 minutes or up to 2 hours before serving.

CHEF'S NOTE: *The cucumber is* partially *peeled in this recipe, mainly for decorative purposes. Do so by scraping "lines" down the length of the cucumber with a peeler to remove very thin strips of the peel.*

CHEF'S NOTE: *If you are using large slices of bread, you may be able to cut 4 rounds out of each bread slice.*

GLUTEN-FREE OPTION

These lovely chickpea sandwiches can serve as full-sized sandwiches or dainty tea sandwiches. Creamy chickpeas paired with the zip of fresh lemon juice provide a pleasing combo that's all dressed up with delicate alfalfa sprouts. These sandwiches make an appetizing and filling luncheon entrée.

PRETTY PAPRIKA-CHICKPEA *Finger Sandwiches*

MAKES 12 TEA SANDWICHES, OR 4 FULL-SIZED SANDWICHES

CHICKPEA SPREAD

1 can (14 to 16 ounces) **chickpeas** (garbanzo beans), **drained and rinsed**

2 tablespoons water, plus more as needed

1½ tablespoons freshly squeezed lemon juice

1½ tablespoons sesame tahini (purchase certified gluten-free tahini if you are gluten-free)

¼ rounded teaspoon smoked paprika

¼ teaspoon sea salt

⅛ teaspoon garlic powder

2 tablespoons seeded and diced mini sweet peppers

SANDWICHES

8 thin slices, vegan whole-grain bread (or vegan *and* gluten-free bread for a gluten-free option)

½ to ¾ cup alfalfa sprouts

2 teaspoons vegan mayonnaise or *Very Delicious Vegan Mayonnaise* (page 83)

GARNISH

12 dill or parsley sprigs

12 mini sweet pepper rings

12 toothpicks

Put the chickpeas, water, lemon juice, tahini, smoked paprika, salt and garlic powder into a medium-sized bowl and mash using a potato masher or large fork until combined, but still chunky. Add a bit more water if the mixture seems too thick to spread. Fold in the diced mini sweet peppers.

To assemble the sandwiches, put 4 bread slices on a cutting board and spread one-quarter of the chickpea spread over each slice. Top with some sprouts. Spread ½ teaspoon vegan mayonnaise on one side of each of the 4 remaining bread slices and top each sandwich with a bread slice, gently pressing down. Using a serrated knife, cut each sandwich into 3 "finger" shapes (see photo, opposite page). Garnish each tiny sandwich with a sprig of dill (or parsley) and a mini pepper ring, secured with a toothpick. Arrange on a pretty platter and serve (see note).

CHEF'S NOTE: *Sandwiches may be assembled and stored, loosely covered, in the refrigerator for up to 1 hour before serving.*

GLUTEN-FREE

This delicious egg-free spread beautifully replaces the traditional recipe. The miso adds a tangy taste, while smoked paprika and turmeric both add color and flavor. If you've recently gone plant-based and are missing this American classic sandwich spread, give mine a try.

VEGAN *Egg Salad* FOR EVERYONE

MAKES 4 SERVINGS

- **1 block** (14 to 16 ounces) **firm or extra-firm regular tofu, well-drained** (see note)
- **½ cup firmly packed shredded carrots** (peeling is optional)
- **⅓ cup of minced green olives, with pimentos or minced black olives**
- **1 teaspoon Italian seasoning blend**
- **3 heaping tablespoons vegan mayonnaise or *Very Delicious Vegan Mayonnaise*** (page 83)
- **1 rounded tablespoon Dijon or spicy brown mustard**
- **1 rounded teaspoon gluten-free mellow white miso**
- **½ teaspoon smoked paprika**
- **¼ teaspoon ground turmeric**
- **⅛ teaspoon sea salt, plus more as needed**
- **Freshly ground black pepper, to taste**

Put the tofu into a medium-sized bowl and mash using a potato masher or large fork until crumbly, but chunks of the tofu remain. Add the carrots, olives and Italian seasoning and stir to combine. Put the vegan mayonnaise, mustard, miso, paprika, turmeric and salt into a small bowl and whisk to combine. Pour the mayo mixture over the tofu and stir to combine. Taste and add some freshly ground black pepper and more salt, if desired. Cover and refrigerate until serving.

CHEF'S NOTE: *If you are cooking gluten free, make certain to purchase certified gluten-free tofu, available in most supermarkets.*

Vegan Egg Salad for Everyone *(page 140), above* Open-Faced Mock "Tuna" Sandwich *(page 142)*, with Spinach and Apple Salad *(page 118), below*

Toasted nori gives this satisfying sandwich a seafood-like taste that makes a crowd-pleasing sandwich, reminiscent of what many of us grew up with.

OPEN-FACED *Mock "Tuna"* SANDWICHES

MAKES 2 SERVINGS

1 block (8 ounces) **gluten-free 3- or 5-grain tempeh, cubed**

1 sheet toasted nori (see note)

2 tablespoons vegan mayonnaise or *Very Delicious Vegan Mayonnaise* (page 83)

1 heaping teaspoon Dijon mustard

1 teaspoon all-purpose seasoning

¼ teaspoon ground turmeric

¼ teaspoon sea salt, plus more as needed

Freshly ground black pepper, to taste

2 large slices vegan whole-grain bread (or vegan *and* gluten-free bread for a gluten-free option)

Sliced tomatoes, if desired

Alfalfa sprouts, if desired

Fit a steamer basket into a medium-sized saucepan with a tight-fitting lid. Add 2 to 3 inches of cold water, and then add the cubed tempeh. Cover and bring to a boil. Steam the tempeh for 10 minutes. Put the steamed tempeh in a medium-sized bowl and mash it just until crumbly, using a potato masher or large fork, and then let it cool for 15 minutes.

Meanwhile, place the nori sheet in a blender and process into coarse crumbs. Add the ground nori, vegan mayonnaise, Dijon mustard, all-purpose seasoning, turmeric and salt to the cooled tempeh and gently stir to combine. Season with pepper and more salt to taste. Cover and refrigerate for 2 to 4 hours, or until completely chilled, before assembling your sandwiches. To make open-faced sandwiches, put a slice of bread on a plate and top with the mock tuna. Garnish with tomatoes and fresh sprouts. Repeat with remaining bread slice and mock tuna and serve!

CHEF'S NOTE: *Found in health food stores or online, toasted nori "sheets" are often sold as "sushi nori." Nori is a sea vegetable most commonly used to hold together sushi rolls, but it's a great way to add a "fish-like" taste to this vegan "tuna."*

See photo of this recipe on page 141.

GLUTEN-FREE OPTION

Here's a jazzy spin on a kids' favorite that's loved by adults, too!

Grilled Cheeze-y AND AVOCADO SANDWICH

MAKES 3 SERVINGS

6 slices vegan whole-grain bread (or vegan *and* gluten-free bread for a gluten-free option)

3 teaspoons vegan buttery spread, plus more as needed

3 teaspoons vegan mayonnaise or *Very Delicious Vegan Mayonnaise* (page 83)

3 to 6 slices mozzarella or cheddar-style vegan cheese (see note)

1 avocado, pitted, peeled and sliced

CHEF'S NOTE: *If you do not have a panini maker, you can make this sandwich in a skillet on the stove. Prepare as instructed, but make certain to weigh down the sandwich with a heavy pan lid while cooking, and flip the sandwich halfway through cooking.*

Preheat a panini maker to 375 degrees F (see note). Thinly spread some vegan buttery spread on one side of each slice of bread. Put one bread slice on a plate ("butter" side down) and spread the other side of the bread slice with a small amount of vegan mayonnaise. Add 1 or 2 vegan cheese slices, and then top with avocado slices and another slice of bread, with the "buttered" side facing upward.

Put 1 or 2 sandwiches in the panini maker. Close the lid and let cook for 3 to 6 minutes (checking often), or until the sandwich is golden brown on the outside, the cheese has melted and the avocado is warmed on the inside. Put the sandwich on a serving plate and let sit for at least 2 minutes, allowing the sandwich to cool slightly. Repeat to make 3 sandwiches in all. Cut each sandwich in half and serve.

CHEF'S NOTE: *If you are cooking gluten free, make certain to purchase certified gluten-free vegan cheese and gluten-free bread, available in many supermarkets.*

See photo of this recipe on page 144.

Grilled Cheeze-y and Avocado Sandwich *(page 143), above*

Reuben-Style Sandwiches *(page 145), below*

These taste so much like the traditional version that they take me back to my childhood in Ohio, where I often ordered this sandwich at the local deli. The dressing that flavors the sandwich is my mom's recipe—I think it's the best *Thousand Island Dressing* around!

Reuben-Style SANDWICHES

MAKES 2 TO 3 SANDWICHES

THOUSAND ISLAND DRESSING

¼ cup vegan mayonnaise or *Very Delicious Vegan Mayonnaise* (page 83)

1 tablespoon sweet pickle relish

1 tablespoon ketchup

2 teaspoons minced scallion, white and green parts

SANDWICHES

¾ to 1 cup sauerkraut

2 to 3 teaspoons vegan buttery spread

4 to 6 slices vegan rye bread

4 to 6 slices vegan cheese

4 to 6 slices vegan deli-style "ham" or slices of *Maple Baked Tofu* (page 220)

To make the dressing, put all the ingredients in a small bowl and whisk to combine. To make the sandwiches, put the sauerkraut in a colander and press firmly with the back of a wooden spoon to extract as much moisture as possible. Spread some vegan buttery spread evenly over one side of each slice of bread.

Place 2 (or 3) of the bread slices, buttery-side down, in a large skillet. Top each with 2 slices of vegan cheese, 2 slices of vegan deli-style "ham" or sliced *Maple Baked Tofu* and some sauerkraut. Spoon 1 to 2 tablespoons of the dressing over the sauerkraut and top with another slice of bread, buttery-side up. Weigh down the sandwiches with a heavy lid or sandwich weight. Cook over medium-low heat until the underside is brown and crispy, about 5 minutes. Flip the sandwiches and cook until the other side is crispy and the vegan cheese is melted. Serve immediately.

GLUTEN-FREE OPTION

When I was a girl, I loved the lox and bagel platter from my local deli. My vegan version surprisingly mimics the taste and texture of the original. I often serve this when I am hosting a breakfast or brunch buffet. It's always a big hit!

Lox-less AND BAGELS

MAKES 4 SERVINGS

- 4 large lettuce leaves
- 4 fresh, vegan whole-grain bagels, split lengthwise (see note for gluten-free option)
- 4 to 6 heaping tablespoons vegan cream cheese
- 2 large tomatoes, sliced
- 1 sweet onion, thinly sliced
- 4 tablespoons capers, drained and rinsed

Put a lettuce leaf on each of four plates. Arrange two halves of a bagel, cut side up on the lettuce leaf. Spread some vegan cream cheese on each bagel half and top with a few tomato slices and some onion slices. Sprinkle ½ tablespoon capers over the top of each bagel half. Serve immediately.

CHEF'S NOTE: *To ensure that your bagels are vegan, purchase bagels that are free of honey, dairy products and eggs. If you want your bagels to be gluten free, too, purchase certified gluten-free, vegan varieties, which are available at some health food stores and for purchase online. If you have difficulty finding vegan and/or gluten-free bagels, try this recipe on whole-grain bread or rolls. It's delicious either way!*

This tantalizing recipe was inspired by the sausage sandwiches served at the annual *Feast of San Gennaro* in lower Manhattan's Little Italy. With its authentic Italian-American taste and colorful presentation, this is a great choice to serve at a family lunch or casual supper.

ITALIAN "SAUSAGE" AND PEPPER *Hoagies*

MAKES 4 TO 5 SERVINGS

1 large sweet onion, thinly sliced

1½ cups vegetable broth, divided, plus more as needed

1 tablespoon extra-virgin olive oil (optional)

1 teaspoon Italian seasoning blend

Scant ⅛ teaspoon cayenne pepper

3 sweet yellow, red and/or orange sweet bell peppers, seeded and sliced

4 large (14 to 16 ounces) **vegan Italian-style sausages or kielbasa, each sliced into 5 to 6 pieces on the diagonal**

4 to 5 vegan hoagie-style rolls, split

Put the onion, 2 tablespoons of broth and optional olive oil in a large skillet. Cook over medium-low heat for 3 minutes. Add the Italian seasoning and cayenne pepper. Cover and cook for 3 minutes, stirring often. Add more broth, 1 tablespoon at a time, as needed to prevent sticking.

Add the peppers, cover and cook, stirring occasionally, for 5 minutes, adding 1 tablespoon of broth at a time as needed to prevent sticking. Add the sausage slices and the remaining broth to the skillet. Cover and cook for about 7 minutes, stirring occasionally, adding more broth if needed. Serve immediately in warm, hoagie-style buns with *All-American Potato Salad* (page 108), if desired.

This savory spread is surprisingly flavorful, using just two ingredients! It makes a satisfying spread for your morning toast or a yummy filling for a satisfying sandwich. Makes a great dip, too!

Avocado-Miso SANDWICH SPREAD

MAKES 2 SERVINGS

1 small, ripe avocado, pitted and peeled

1 heaping teaspoon gluten-free mellow white miso

Put the avocado in a small bowl and add the mellow white miso. Vigorously stir to combine. Serve immediately.

Rock-n-roll legend has it that the King of Rock, Elvis Presley, loved fried peanut butter and banana sandwiches. I have always liked the combination of peanut butter and bananas myself, and this healthy version of the king's favorite snack is a great option for an on-the-go lunch!

Rockin' PEANUT BUTTER-BANANA TOAST

MAKES 2 SERVINGS

2 large slices vegan whole-grain bread, toasted (use vegan *and* gluten-free bread for a gluten-free option)

4 tablespoons creamy or chunky peanut butter (see note)

2 small bananas, peeled and sliced

Put each slice of toast on a plate. Spread each toast slice with 2 tablespoons of peanut butter. Arrange the slices from 1 banana over the top of the peanut butter, in an even layer. Serve immediately.

CHEF'S NOTE: *For a fresh twist, try substituting almond, sunflower seed, hazelnut, cashew or your favorite nut (or seed) butter in place of the peanut butter.*

These versatile roll-ups are perfect for any midday meal, from a casual brunch to an elegant luncheon. They also travel well, making them ideal for packed lunches or picnics. Just wrap them in parchment paper and go!

Hummus-Avocado ROLLS WITH SUNFLOWER SEEDS

MAKES 2 SERVINGS

2 vegan whole-grain flour tortillas or wraps (or vegan *and* gluten-free tortillas for a gluten-free option)

2 to 4 tablespoons store-bought hummus or *Turmeric-Lemon Hummus* (page 62)

2 rounded teaspoons vegan mayonnaise or *Very Delicious Vegan Mayonnaise* (page 83)

4 ounces (about 5 cups, lightly packed) **mixed baby greens**

1 avocado, peeled, pitted and sliced

8 small green or black olives, pitted and chopped

2 teaspoons raw or roasted sunflower seeds

Lay the tortillas on a large cutting board. Spread 1 or 2 tablespoons of the hummus evenly over half of each tortilla. Spread 1 rounded teaspoon of vegan mayonnaise evenly over the other half of each tortilla. Evenly arrange one-half of the greens, avocado, olives and sunflower seeds over the lower two-thirds of each wrap. Starting at the bottom edge, roll the tortilla tightly and evenly around the filling. Gently (but firmly) press the edge to seal the roll. Set the roll seam-side down, cut it diagonally into 3 to 4 pieces and serve.

Impossible as it sounds, the year of the vegan burger is finally here! In this chapter I have made it easy for you to serve your family a delicious variety of freshly prepared plant-based burgers. From bean burgers to nut burgers, zucchini-based burgers, portobello mushroom burgers and more, you'll be surprised at the wide range of *jazzylicious* burgers that can be created in your own home kitchen. No "take-out" required!

CHAPTER

TEN

The Burger Joint

Mushroom-Nut Burgers, *page 160*

These moist and dense burgers stand in pleasingly for a traditional burger, featuring the hearty texture of red beans along with other nutritious goodies. I like to serve these with smoky *Pink Paprika Sauce* (page 87) drizzled over the burger or on the side.

RED BEAN *Burgers*

MAKES 6 SERVINGS

1½ tablespoons plus 2 teaspoons extra-virgin olive oil, divided

1 can (15 to 16 ounces) **red kidney beans, drained and rinsed**

3 tablespoons ketchup

½ teaspoon smoked paprika

¼ teaspoon sea salt

1½ cups freshly ground vegan whole-grain bread crumbs (use vegan *and* gluten-free bread for a gluten-free option) (see note, page 160)

½ cup gluten-free, quick cooking rolled oats

4 tablespoons firmly packed, shredded zucchini

Preheat the oven to 375 degrees F. Line a large, rimmed baking pan with unbleached parchment paper. Lightly coat the parchment paper with 2 teaspoons of olive oil. Put the kidney beans, ketchup, 1½ tablespoons olive oil, smoked paprika and salt into a medium-sized bowl and mash together using a potato masher or large fork, until most of the beans are mashed. Fold in the bread crumbs, rolled oats and zucchini and stir together with a large spoon to combine.

To form a burger, scoop up a rounded ⅓ cup of the mixture using a measuring cup. Firmly pack the burger mixture into the measuring cup and drop it onto the lined pan. Gently press the burger using a flat spatula to form it into the shape of a burger. Continue in this manner until you have formed a total of 6 burgers. Tent with foil and bake for 18 minutes. Remove the foil and flip the burgers over. Bake uncovered for an additional 10 to 20 minutes or until the burgers are golden around the edges and firming up. Transfer the pan to a wire rack and let cool 10 minutes. (The burgers may still be a bit soft, so handle them carefully.) Serve the burgers with *Cucumber, Tomato and Mini-Pepper Salad* (page 115), *Tiny Potatoes with Spicy Mustard Sauce* (page 243) and *Pink Paprika Sauce* (page 87) on the side (see note).

CHEF'S NOTE: *My husband likes a* Double Red Bean Burger *(pictured here). To serve this "take-out" style double-decker sandwich, start with a slice of whole-grain (or gluten-free) bread and top with a large leaf of romaine lettuce, a spoonful of* Pink Paprika Sauce *(page 87), a burger patty, shredded vegan cheese, thick slice of sweet onion, another burger patty, a bit more vegan cheese, more sauce and a few mini sweet pepper rings. Top it all with another slice of bread, then garnish (optional) with a basil leaf and a cherry tomato—all held together with a small skewer. Incredibly good!*

Filled with super nutritious foods like white beans, whole grains, zucchini and seeds, these burgers are truly a powerful way to serve an American classic.

Powerhouse BURGERS

MAKES 8 SERVINGS

2 tablespoons plus 2 teaspoons extra-virgin olive oil, divided, plus more as needed

1 can (15 to 16 ounces) **white cannellini beans, drained, rinsed and mashed**

1 cup firmly packed shredded zucchini (from about 1 small zucchini)

1 cup firmly packed, freshly ground vegan whole-grain bread crumbs (use vegan *and* gluten-free bread for a gluten-free option) (see note, page 160)

1½ teaspoons smoked paprika

1 teaspoon all-purpose seasoning

1 teaspoon garlic powder

½ teaspoon sea salt, plus more as needed

½ cup roasted and salted sunflower seeds

3 tablespoons ketchup

2 tablespoons gluten-free, quick cooking rolled oats

2 tablespoons toasted wheat germ (use gluten-free oat bran for a gluten-free option)

Line a large, rimmed baking pan with unbleached parchment paper. Lightly coat the parchment paper with 2 teaspoons of olive oil. Put the mashed cannellini beans into a medium-sized bowl. Add the shredded zucchini and mix together with a large spoon to combine. Put the bread crumbs, smoked paprika, all-purpose seasoning, garlic powder and ½ teaspoon sea salt into another medium-sized bowl and stir to combine. Add the bread crumb mixture to the cannellini beans and stir to combine.

Put the sunflower seeds into a blender or food processor and process into coarse crumbs. Transfer the ground sunflower seeds to the cannellini bean mixture. Add the ketchup, rolled oats, wheat germ (or gluten-free oat bran) and 1 tablespoon olive oil and stir to thoroughly combine.

To form a burger, scoop up ⅓ cup of the mixture using a measuring cup. Firmly pack the burger mixture into the measuring cup and drop it onto the lined pan. Gently press the mixture using a flat spatula to form it into the shape of a burger. Continue in this manner until you have formed a total of 8 burgers. Put the pan into the refrigerator for 1 to 2 hours to allow the burgers to firm up. When you're ready to bake the burgers, preheat the oven to 375 degrees F. Brush a scant ½ teaspoon of olive oil over the top of each burger. Bake the burgers for 20 minutes. Remove the burgers from the oven and flip them. Increase the heat to 400 degrees F and bake for 10 to 15 minutes more or until they are firm, slightly crispy and golden on each side. Put the pan on a wire rack and sprinkle sea salt over the top of the burgers, if desired. Let cool for 5 minutes and serve (see note).

CHEF'S NOTE: *To serve the burger as pictured here, start with a crusty bun or roll (or gluten-free bun or roll) and spread with a bit of* Creamy Paprika Sauce *(page 86), and then top with baby greens or baby spinach. Add the burger, 1 large slice of tomato, 1 large slice of sweet onion and several mini sweet pepper rings. Spread some of the sauce on the underside of the remaining bun half and place it on top of the burger. Yummy!*

GLUTEN-FREE OPTION

My husband always complained that I did not make our veggie burgers BIG enough! So the *"Hungry Guy" Burger* was born. This has become a real fan favorite, packed with hearty black beans, spicy salsa and rolled oats. Plus, these five-ingredient wonders are super-quick to prepare *and* super delish. Now everyone's happy!

"Hungry Guy" BURGERS

MAKES 6 SERVINGS

1 can (15 to 16 ounces) **black beans, drained and rinsed**

⅔ cup plus 2 heaping tablespoons prepared salsa, plus more as needed (see note)

3 slices vegan whole-grain or gluten-free bread, torn into chunks

¼ teaspoon ground cumin

⅔ cup gluten-free, old fashioned rolled oats

Preheat the oven to 375 degrees F. Line a large, rimmed baking pan with unbleached parchment paper. Put the black beans and salsa in a medium-sized bowl and mash using a potato masher or large fork until well combined. Put the bread chunks and cumin in a blender and process into coarse crumbs. Add the bread crumbs to the black bean mixture and stir to combine. Stir in the rolled oats and mix to combine. If the mixture seems dry, stir in another heaping tablespoon of salsa and mix to combine.

Scoop up a generous ½ cup of the black bean mixture and put it on the prepared pan. Form it into a burger, shaping it with clean hands, and then flatten it slightly. Continue in this manner until you have formed a total of 6 burgers (see note). Bake for 20 minutes. Flip the burgers and bake for 8 to 12 minutes or until golden.

CHEF'S NOTE: *You may use mild, medium or hot salsa in this recipe.*

CHEF'S NOTE: *Once formed, the burgers may be covered and refrigerated for 2 to 6 hours before cooking. Add 5 to 7 minutes to the baking time.*

Photo courtesy of Annie Olivero. Learn more about Annie on page 296.

GLUTEN-FREE OPTION

This snazzy burger is an updated version of my original well-loved *Mushroom-Nut Burger* recipe. Packed with flavorful ingredients, it also has a "meaty" texture. This burger is a sure winner! Bonus—these burgers freeze well too!

MUSHROOM-NUT *Burgers*

MAKES 4 SERVINGS

- **1½ cups freshly ground vegan whole-grain bread crumbs** (use vegan *and* gluten-free bread for a gluten-free option) (see note)
- **1 teaspoon Italian seasoning blend**
- **½ teaspoon chili powder**
- **½ teaspoon garlic powder**
- **⅛ teaspoon sea salt**
- **½ cup chopped walnuts**
- **2 cups chopped cremini or white button mushrooms**
- **⅓ cup diced sweet onion**
- **1 teaspoon gluten-free tamari**
- **¼ cup vital wheat gluten** (optional, omit for a gluten-free option, see note)
- **1 tablespoon extra-virgin olive oil, plus more as needed**

CHEF'S NOTE: *Freshly made bread crumbs* must *be used in this recipe, as dry bread crumbs will not hold the burgers together. To make fresh bread crumbs, tear 3 to 4 slices of fresh, soft, whole-grain (or gluten-free) bread into chunks. Put the bread chunks into a blender and process (on low) into coarse crumbs.*

Preheat the oven to 375 degrees F. Line a medium-sized baking pan with unbleached parchment paper.

Put the bread crumbs, Italian seasoning, chili powder, garlic powder and salt into a large bowl. Put the walnuts in a blender and process until coarsely ground. Add the walnuts to the bread crumb mixture and stir to incorporate. Put the mushrooms, onion and tamari in a blender and process into a chunky purée. Add the mushroom mixture to the walnut/bread crumb mixture and stir to incorporate. Stir in the optional wheat gluten and 1 tablespoon olive oil, adding more olive oil 1 teaspoon at a time, if needed, until wheat gluten is fully incorporated and the mixture is no longer dry and holds together when held in the palm of your hand.

Place a 3½ to 4-inch cookie cutter ring on the parchment. Pack one-quarter of the mushroom–bread crumb mixture into the ring and press it firmly and evenly into the ring to form a "burger." Gently remove the ring (see note). Repeat with the remaining mushroom/bread crumb mixture until you have formed a total of 4 burgers. Flatten each burger slightly with the back of a flat spatula.

CHEF'S NOTE: *Alternately, you may form 4 burgers by hand and then flatten each burger slightly with the back of a flat spatula.*

Bake for 15 minutes. Flip each burger and bake for an additional 15 to 18 minutes or until the burgers are

slightly crisp and golden. Serve with *Ketchup-Mayo Sauce* (page 87) in a whole-grain (or gluten-free) bun, along with a thick slice of tomato, chopped sweet onion, dill pickle slices and crisp romaine lettuce (see photo) for an "out of this world" veggie burger!

CHEF'S NOTE: *The addition of the vital wheat gluten will produce a firmer burger with a more realistic "burger" texture. That being said, I have made these burgers* many times *without the wheat gluten and love them* just as much *that way! So–in short–the vital wheat gluten is* truly optional! *If you* do *omit the wheat gluten, decrease the amount of olive oil to 1 to 2 teaspoons. (If you are cooking gluten free, be certain to omit the vital wheat gluten.)*

Tired of frozen meat-free burgers? These burgers bring a ray of sunshine to your table, with protein-rich ingredients like black beans, sunflower seeds and walnuts. These patties prep for the oven in less than 10 minutes, making them an ideal option for a casual weeknight meal.

Sunny BLACK BEAN BURGERS

MAKES 6 SERVINGS

½ cup roasted and salted sunflower seeds

½ cup chopped walnuts

1 cup lightly packed, freshly ground vegan whole-grain bread crumbs (use vegan *and* gluten-free bread for a gluten-free option) (see note, page 160)

2 teaspoons extra-virgin olive oil, plus more as needed

1 can (15 to 16 ounces) **black beans, drained and rinsed**

5 tablespoons vegan marinara sauce, plus more as needed

3 tablespoons minced sweet onion

½ teaspoon garlic powder

½ teaspoon Italian seasoning blend

CHEF'S NOTE: *Not all vegan marinara sauce is gluten free. Purchase certified gluten-free sauce if you are gluten free.*

Line a medium-sized baking pan with unbleached parchment paper. Put the sunflower seeds into a blender and process into coarse crumbs. Transfer to a small bowl. Put the walnuts into a blender, process into coarse crumbs and add them to the sunflower seeds. Add the bread crumbs to the sunflower seed/walnut mixture and mix together using a large spoon. Pour in the olive oil and stir to combine, adding a bit more olive oil if the mixture seems dry.

Put the black beans, marinara sauce, onion, garlic powder and Italian seasoning into a medium-sized bowl and lightly mash, using a potato masher or large fork. Stir in the nut/bread crumb mixture and mix together until well combined, adding a bit more marinara sauce if the mixture seems dry. The mixture should hold together when gathered in the palm of your hand. To form a burger, scoop up a scant ½ cup of the mixture and drop it onto the lined pan. Gently form it into the shape of a burger. Continue in this manner until you have formed a total of 6 burgers. Refrigerate for about 30 minutes (or up to 2 hours) to allow the burgers to firm up.

Preheat the oven to 375 degrees F. Bake for 30 to 35 minutes or until slightly golden, flipping the burgers half way through cooking. Put the pan on a wire rack and let cool for 5 to 10 minutes before serving. (These burgers will be soft, so handle them carefully!) Serve on whole-grain or gluten-free burger buns, with lettuce and tomatoes, topped with *Quick Marinara-Mayo Sauce* (page 87, see variation).

GLUTEN-FREE OPTION

These hearty burger patties are simple to make using leftover rice. Tasting like a cross between falafel and a veggie burger, they make a nice luncheon entrée or light supper.

Quick CHICKPEA-RICE BURGERS

MAKES 6 TO 7 SERVINGS

BREADING

1 cup lightly packed, freshly ground vegan whole-grain bread crumbs (use vegan *and* gluten-free bread for a gluten-free option) (see note, page 160)

2 teaspoons extra-virgin olive oil

¼ teaspoon sea salt

BURGERS

1 can (15 to 16 ounces) **chickpeas** (garbanzo beans), **drained and rinsed**

1 cup firmly packed *cooked* short-grain brown rice

2 tablespoons ketchup

1 teaspoon chili powder

1 cup lightly packed, freshly ground vegan whole-grain bread crumbs (use vegan *and* gluten-free bread for a gluten-free option) (see note, page 160)

Preheat the oven to 400 degrees F. Line a large, rimmed baking pan with unbleached parchment paper. To make the breading, put 1 cup bread crumbs, 2 teaspoons olive oil and sea salt in a small bowl and stir to combine.

To make the burgers, put the chickpeas, brown rice, ketchup and chili powder in a large bowl and coarsely mash with a potato masher or large fork. Add 1 cup bread crumbs and stir until incorporated. Scoop up a rounded ⅓ cup of the chickpea mixture and form it into a burger shape. Dip it in the breading mixture to thoroughly coat. Put the patty on the lined baking pan. Continue in this manner to form a total of 6 to 7 burgers. Tent loosely with foil and bake for 25 minutes. Flip the burger and tent again. Bake for 15 minutes more. Remove the foil and bake for 3 to 5 minutes or until the burgers are crispy and golden. Put the pan on a wire rack and let cool 5 minutes. The burgers will be soft. To serve, carefully transfer the burgers onto serving plates. Serve with a salad and *Classic Cocktail Sauce* (page 88).

GLUTEN-FREE OPTION

These flavorsome meatless patties feature tofu, carrots and spices. They are convenient to prepare for a weeknight meal, using ingredients you probably already have on hand.

Tofulicious PATTY

MAKES 4 TO 6 SERVINGS

1½ tablespoons plus 2 teaspoons extra-virgin olive oil, divided

1 block (14 to 16 ounces) **extra-firm regular tofu, drained well and crumbled** (see note)

1 tablespoon Dijon or spicy brown mustard

1 tablespoon gluten-free tamari

½ teaspoon smoked paprika

½ cup firmly packed shredded carrots (peeling is optional)

1⅓ cups lightly packed, freshly ground vegan whole-grain bread crumbs (use vegan *and* gluten-free bread for a gluten-free option) (see note, page 160)

CHEF'S NOTE: *If you are cooking gluten free, make certain to purchase certified gluten-free tofu, available in most supermarkets.*

Line a large, rimmed baking pan with unbleached parchment paper. Lightly coat the parchment paper with 2 teaspoons of olive oil. Put the tofu, 1 tablespoon olive oil, mustard, tamari and smoked paprika into a large bowl. Mash together using a potato masher or large fork until combined. Add the shredded carrots and stir together, using a large spoon. Add the bread crumbs and remaining ½ tablespoon olive oil and mix to combine.

Scoop up a generous ⅓ to ½ cup of the tofu mixture (depending upon how large you would like your patties to be) and firmly press the tofu mixture into the cup. Put it on the prepared pan and form it into a burger, shaping it with clean hands, and then flatten it to about ½-inch thickness, using a flat spatula. Make 4 to 6 patties in this manner. Tent the patties with foil and refrigerate for 1 to 2 hours to firm up.

Preheat the oven to 400 degrees F. Bake the tofu patties for 30 minutes, and then flip them and bake uncovered for an additional 20 minutes or until golden brown. Transfer the pan to a wire rack and let cool for 10 minutes. (These patties will be *very* soft, almost like croquettes). Serve the patties warm, over a green salad.

GLUTEN-FREE

These enticing "burgers" are simple to prepare but they're packed with juicy flavor. When you crave a meaty tasting burger, this recipe fills the bill.

Crazy Easy BBQ PORTOBELLO BURGERS

MAKES 6 SERVINGS

6 large portobello mushrooms, cleaned and stems removed

1½ tablespoons extra-virgin olive oil

½ tablespoon gluten-free tamari

½ cup vegan barbecue sauce or *Easiest BBQ Sauce* (page 90)**, plus more as needed**

Line a large, rimmed baking pan with unbleached parchment paper. Arrange the portobello mushrooms gill side up on the prepared pan. Spoon about one-sixth of the olive oil and one-sixth of the tamari over the gills of each mushroom cap. Tent the mushrooms with foil, and if time permits, refrigerate for 30 minutes to let the flavors marry.

Preheat the oven to 375 degrees F. Bake the mushrooms for 30 minutes. Transfer the pan to a wire rack and remove the foil. Gently flip the mushrooms over so the smooth side of the cap is facing up. Spread a scant tablespoon of barbecue sauce evenly over the top of each mushroom. Bake uncovered for 15 minutes. Remove the mushrooms from the oven and add another teaspoon or so of the barbecue sauce to each mushroom. Bake for an additional 12 to 15 minutes or until the mushrooms have become caramelized and the edges are browned.

Serve over a crisp green salad or serve in a whole-grain (or gluten-free) bun, (pictured on opposite page) with *Creamy Paprika Sauce* (page 86), lettuce, sweet onion and tomato, if desired.

GLUTEN-FREE OPTION

I used to love crab cakes, and creating a vegan version was high on my recipe "to-do" list for quite a while. So imagine my happy dance when I came up with this delicious adaptation that's so easy to prepare! These patties make an appetizing first course or main dish for any special meal, served with *Classic Cocktail Sauce* (page 88) on the side.

Not-So-Crabby CAKES

MAKES 4 TO 8 SERVINGS

"CRABBY" CAKES

2¼ cups lightly packed, freshly ground vegan bread crumbs (use vegan *and* gluten-free bread for a gluten-free option) (see note, page 160)

1 teaspoon dry mustard powder

½ teaspoon dried marjoram

¼ teaspoon sea salt

¼ teaspoon cayenne pepper (use ⅛ teaspoon for less heat)

¼ teaspoon dulse flakes or granules (optional, see note)

1 cup firmly packed grated zucchini

½ cup minced sweet onion

3 heaping tablespoons sesame tahini, plus more as needed (purchase certified gluten-free tahini if you are gluten-free)

BREADING

⅔ cup lightly packed, freshly ground vegan bread crumbs (use vegan *and* gluten-free bread for a gluten-free option)

2 teaspoons extra-virgin olive oil, plus more as needed

¼ teaspoon sea salt

Preheat the oven to 400 degrees F. Line a large, rimmed baking sheet with unbleached parchment paper. To make the cakes, put 2¼ cups bread crumbs, mustard powder, marjoram, ¼ teaspoon sea salt, cayenne pepper and dulse (optional) in a large bowl and stir with a large spoon to combine. Add the zucchini and onion and stir to combine. Add the tahini and stir until incorporated. If the mixture seems dry, add 1 more tablespoon of tahini.

CHEF'S NOTE: *If you cannot find dulse flakes or granules, you may use toasted nori sheets instead. Put a ½ sheet of toasted nori into a blender and grind into coarse crumbs. Proceed with recipe as directed.*

To make the breading, put ⅔ cup bread crumbs, 2 teaspoons olive oil and ¼ teaspoon sea salt in a small bowl and stir to combine. Add an additional teaspoon of olive oil if the bread crumbs seem dry.

Scoop up ¼ cup of the zucchini mixture and form it into a cake. Dip it in the breading mixture to thoroughly coat all sides. Put the "crabby" cake on the prepared baking sheet and gently press down to compress it slightly. (This will help it to hold together while baking.) Continue in this manner to form a total of 8 cakes. Tent loosely with foil and bake for 20 to 25 minutes or until the cakes are starting to firm up. Flip and re-tent with foil. Bake for 10 to 15 minutes more, or until edges are golden. Remove the foil and bake for another 5

to 7 minutes or until the cakes are crispy. Put the sheet on a wire rack and let cool 5 minutes. The cakes will be soft.

To serve, carefully transfer the cakes onto individual serving plates. For an appetizer, serve 1 cake per person; for a main course, serve 2 to 3 cakes per person, with *Classic Cocktail Sauce* (page 88) on the side and garnished with a lemon wedge, if desired.

This chapter celebrates exciting ways to change up "pasta night." From zoodles to veggie "noodles" to oodles of tasty alternatives, you'll be amazed as to how these recipes really look *and* taste like traditional, wheat-based spaghetti, fettuccine, lasagna and more! Oh—did I mention? All of the sauces in this chapter are equally *jazzylicious* served over traditional wheat-based or gluten-free noodle varieties, too. So whether you're looking for gluten-free dishes or just want to "lighten up" spaghetti suppers, these pasta impostors are sure to please!

CHAPTER

ELEVEN

Pasta Impostors

Spaghetti Squash "Capellini" with Sweet Pepper Marinara Sauce, *page 181*

This easy recipe makes a pleasing pasta substitute for a weeknight meal. *Al dente* summer squash "noodles" topped with a zippy caper-tomato sauce has a whole *lotta* flavor, but very few ingredients. That's *easy* Italian!

EASY CAPER-TOMATO SAUCE WITH YELLOW SQUASH Linguine

MAKES 4 SERVINGS

- 1 small yellow onion, diced
- 2 tablespoons extra-virgin olive oil, divided, plus more as needed
- 1 tablespoon gluten-free tamari
- ⅛ teaspoon crushed red pepper
- 1 can (24 to 28 ounces) fire roasted diced tomatoes, with juice (see note)
- 3 tablespoons nonpareil capers, drained
- ½ cup plus 2 tablespoons chopped fresh parsley, divided
- 3 medium-large yellow summer squash

Put the onion, 1 tablespoon olive oil, tamari and crushed red pepper in a large saucepan. Cover and cook for 7 minutes over medium heat, stirring occasionally. Decrease the heat to medium-low and add the fire roasted tomatoes (with juice) and capers. Cover and cook for 45 to 55 minutes or until the sauce is thickened, stirring occasionally. Stir in ½ cup of parsley and cook for 5 minutes.

While the sauce cooks, use a vegetable peeler spiralizer (or regular spiralizer) to shave the summer squash into linguine-style "noodles." When the sauce is cooked, put the squash linguine into a large, nonstick sauté pan and add 1 tablespoon of olive oil. Cover and cook over medium heat, stirring often, for about 3 minutes. Add 2 tablespoons parsley and cook 3 to 4 minutes more, or until the squash linguine is cooked *al dente*. Arrange some squash linguine on each of four serving plates and top with caper-tomato sauce. Serve immediately.

CHEF'S NOTE: *For a thicker sauce, use canned fire roasted* crushed *tomatoes.*

GLUTEN-FREE

This pasta-licious recipe is a *true* pasta impostor. My husband says it tastes *just* like a rich, cream-laden spaghetti dish. When I served it recently to my mom and stepdad, they both *insisted* there was wheat spaghetti mixed in with the zucchini "fettucine!" I must say: I love this dish, and I think you and your family will, too!

ZUCCHINI FETTUCCINE Alfredo

MAKES 2 TO 3 SERVINGS

- ⅔ cup raw cashews
- ⅔ cup plus 2 tablespoons water, divided
- 1 heaping teaspoon gluten-free mellow white miso
- 2 teaspoons freshly squeezed lemon juice
- 1/16 rounded teaspoon garlic powder
- ⅛ heaping teaspoon salt (see note)
- Freshly ground black pepper, to taste
- 3 large (or 4 medium) zucchini
- 1 tablespoon extra-virgin olive oil

Put the cashews in a small bowl and top with ⅓ cup water. Put the cashews and water in the refrigerator and let them soak for 1 to 4 hours. Drain the cashews and rinse thoroughly in cold water. Put the soaked cashews, ½ cup water, miso, lemon juice, garlic powder, salt and pepper into a blender and process for 30 seconds to 1 minute or until *very* smooth and creamy.

To make the "fettuccine," use a vegetable peeler spiralizer (or regular spiralizer) to shave the zucchini into long fettuccine-style "noodles." Put the zucchini fettuccine into a large, nonstick sauté pan and add 1 tablespoon of olive oil. Cook the zucchini over medium heat, stirring often, for 2 to 3 minutes or until *almost* soft. Carefully add three-quarters of the cashew sauce and cook for 2 to 3 minutes, gently stirring using tongs, until the sauce is heated through and the zucchini is cooked *al dente*. (Do not over-cook, or the zucchini "fettuccine" will be mushy!) Add more sauce if a creamier consistency is desired (see note). Serve immediately with any remaining sauce served in a pitcher to pass around the table.

CHEF'S NOTE: *This sauce (uncooked) doubles as a creamy salad dressing. Covered tightly and stored in the refrigerator, leftover sauce will keep for 2 to 3 days.*

CHEF'S NOTE: *For a saltier taste, use ¼ teaspoon salt in this recipe.*

Bathed in a quick-to-make delicious mushroom marinara sauce, these zucchini "noodles," otherwise known as "zoodles," flawlessly take the place of classic spaghetti marinara. Try it. You're gonna love it!

Zoodles MARINARA

MAKES 4 SERVINGS

- 1 large sweet onion, sliced
- 1 tablespoon extra-virgin olive oil
- 1 tablespoon gluten-free tamari
- 8 ounces cremini mushrooms, sliced
- 1 teaspoon Italian seasoning blend
- ¾ teaspoon garlic powder
- ⅛ teaspoon crushed red pepper
- 1 can (24 to 28 ounces) crushed tomatoes
- 1 teaspoon maple syrup
- 9 to 10 cups zucchini "zoodles" (see note)
- 3 tablespoons chopped fresh basil
- 4 basil springs, for garnish (optional)

Put the onion, olive oil and tamari in a large skillet. Cover and cook for 5 minutes over medium heat, stirring occasionally. Add the mushrooms, Italian seasoning, garlic powder and crushed red pepper. Cover and cook for 5 minutes or until the mushrooms are starting to become golden around the edges. Add the tomatoes and maple syrup. Decrease the heat to medium-low, cover and cook for 40 to 45 minutes or until the sauce is thickened, stirring occasionally.

Add the "zoodles," and using tongs, gently incorporate the "zoodles" into the sauce. Cover and cook for 4 to 6 minutes or until the "zoodles" are cooked but still *al dente*. Add the chopped basil and cook for 30 seconds. Divide onto four dinner plates. Decorate each with a sprig of basil and serve.

CHEF'S NOTE: *To make zucchini "noodles" (zoodles) start with 2 to 4 medium to large zucchini. Using a vegetable peeler spiralizer (or regular spiralizer), shave the zucchini into long spaghetti-like strands or "zoodles."*

GLUTEN-FREE

This raw impostor is low in calories, a breeze to prepare and makes fabulous fare on a hot summer night. The zucchini strips really do look and taste a lot like freshly made, chilled pappardelle noodles.

ZUCCHINI *Pappardelle* WITH FRESH TOMATO SALSA

MAKES 3 TO 4 SERVINGS

- 2 medium/large zucchini
- 2 medium ripe tomatoes, chopped
- 10 to 14 leaves fresh basil, minced
- 1 tablespoon extra-virgin olive oil, plus more as needed
- 1 to 2 small cloves garlic, minced
- ¼ teaspoon sea salt, plus more as needed
- Freshly ground black pepper

Shave the zucchini lengthwise with a wide vegetable peeler to resemble pappardelle pasta. Put the zucchini pappardelle in a large bowl. Add the tomatoes, basil, oil, garlic and salt and toss gently using tongs until thoroughly combined. Add more olive oil, if desired. Season with salt and pepper to taste. Serve immediately.

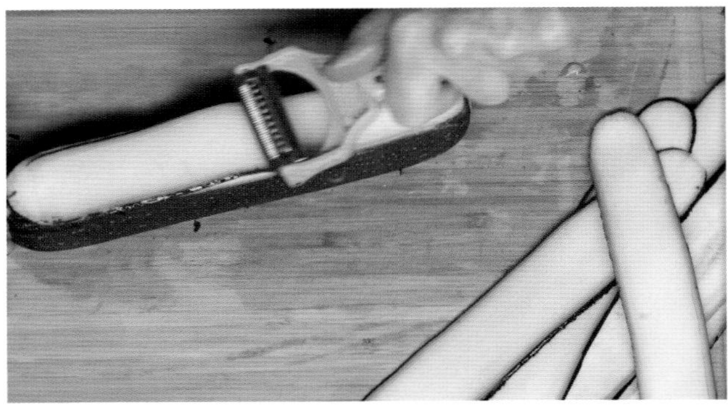

GLUTEN-FREE

The combination of roasted squash smothered in a hearty, homemade marinara sauce makes a delicious entrée. Lighter in calories than traditional pasta but super satisfying, give this one a try when you want to serve an impressive alternative to the classic dish. (This is the *only* way I can get my husband to eat spaghetti squash!)

SPAGHETTI SQUASH "Capellini" with Sweet Pepper Marinara Sauce

MAKES 4 TO 5 SERVINGS

- 1 medium to large spaghetti squash, sliced in half lengthwise
- 2 tablespoons plus 2 teaspoons extra-virgin olive oil, divided
- Sea salt, to taste
- Freshly ground black pepper, to taste
- 1 large sweet onion, thinly sliced
- 1½ tablespoons gluten-free tamari
- 1½ teaspoons Italian seasoning blend, divided
- ½ cup plus 2 tablespoons water, plus more as needed
- 1 medium red or orange sweet bell pepper, seeded and chopped
- 1 can (26 to 28 ounces) crushed tomatoes (fire-roasted are nice)
- Scant ⅛ teaspoon crushed red pepper
- Parsley sprigs or chopped basil, for garnish (optional)

(Recipe continues on page 182.)

To prepare the spaghetti squash, preheat the oven to 400 degrees F. Line a medium-sized rimmed baking pan with unbleached parchment paper. Using a grapefruit spoon or sturdy teaspoon, scoop out the seeds and stringy flesh from the inside of the squash. Season *each* squash half with 1 teaspoon olive oil. Add a liberal amount of salt and pepper to taste. Arrange the spaghetti squash halves cut side down on the prepared pan and bake for 45 minutes to 1 hour (see note), or until the outside of the squash is *very* soft to the touch and the inside edge of each squash half is golden. Put the pan on a wire rack and let the squash cool for at least 20 minutes.

CHEF'S NOTE: *The baking time for the squash will vary depending upon the size of the squash.*

Meanwhile, to make the sauce, put the onion and 2 tablespoons olive oil into a large sauté pan and cook over medium-high heat for 1 minute. Decrease the heat to medium. Add the tamari and 1 teaspoon Italian seasoning, cover and cook for 3 minutes or until the onion becomes translucent, adding 2 tablespoons of water if the pan becomes dry. Add the bell pepper and cook for 5 minutes, stirring occasionally. Add the tomatoes, crushed red pepper and remaining ½ teaspoon Italian seasoning. Pour ½ cup water into the tomato can and slosh it around to loosen the remaining crushed tomatoes. Add the "tomato water" to the pan. Decrease the

heat to medium-low. Cover and cook, stirring occasionally, for 40 to 55 minutes or until the sauce has cooked down and is thickened.

Once the sauce is cooked and the outside of the squash is cool to the touch, scoop out the spaghetti squash strands, breaking them up with a fork to resemble cooked spaghetti (or capellini), and arrange the strands on individual serving plates. Spoon a generous amount of the marinara sauce over each serving of squash, garnish with optional parsley or basil and serve.

When we lived in New Jersey, every August we were blessed with loads of summer squash from our farmer friends. Here's a fresh way to use this tasty and nutritionally dense, late season squash, and the veggie "noodles" make it a welcome alternative to a green salad.

SQUASH AND CARROT "Pasta" Salad

MAKES 2 TO 3 SERVINGS

SALAD

1 medium yellow summer squash or zucchini

1 medium carrot

DRESSING

2 teaspoons vegan mayonnaise or ***Very Delicious Vegan Mayonnaise*** (page 83)

1 small clove garlic, minced

1 teaspoon Dijon mustard

1 teaspoon Italian seasoning blend (see note)

Sea salt, to taste

Freshly ground black pepper, to taste

Shave the squash *and* the carrot lengthwise into thin, long strips using a wide vegetable peeler. Put the squash and carrot strips in a medium-sized bowl.

To make the dressing, put the vegan mayonnaise, garlic, Dijon mustard and Italian seasoning in a small bowl and whisk to combine. Add the dressing to the squash and carrots and gently toss to coat. Season with salt and pepper to taste. Serve at room temperature or cover and refrigerate up to 4 hours and serve cold. Makes a great first course!

CHEF'S NOTE: *You may substitute 1 tablespoon chopped fresh basil in place of the Italian seasoning.*

GLUTEN-FREE OPTION

No wheat-based noodles here, so this is perfect if you are seeking a fresh twist on vegan lasagna. This casserole is a delight to serve at summer's end when nights are cooler and yellow summer squash is widely available from the farm market. Bonus: beets, sunflower seeds and walnuts mixed with a few pantry staples stand in beautifully for the meat in this satisfying main dish.

SUMMER *Lasagna* WITH CASHEW RICOTTA

MAKES 4 TO 6 SERVINGS

SQUASH "LASAGNA NOODLES"

2 large and long yellow summer squash

"MEATY" LAYER

3 slices vegan whole-grain bread (use gluten-free variety for a gluten-free option)

1 tablespoon Italian seasoning blend

¼ teaspoon sea salt

½ cup chopped walnuts

⅓ cup raw sunflower seeds

¾ cup peeled and grated raw beets

CASHEW-BEAN CHEESE LAYER

1 can (15 to 16 ounces) white beans, drained and rinsed

¼ cup chopped fresh basil or 2 teaspoons dried basil

½ teaspoon garlic powder

¼ teaspoon sea salt

½ cup raw cashews

⅓ cup water

ADDITIONAL INGREDIENTS

1⅔ cups of vegan marinara sauce, plus more as needed

2 tablespoons chopped fresh basil, plus more for garnish

Preheat the oven to 400 degrees F. To make the squash lasagna "noodles," slice each squash lengthwise into ⅛-inch thick strips using a very sharp knife.

To make the "meaty" layer, put the bread, Italian seasoning and ¼ teaspoon sea salt into a blender and process into coarse crumbs. Transfer the crumb mixture to a medium-sized bowl. Put the walnuts and sunflower seeds in the blender and process into coarse crumbs. Add the walnuts to the bread crumbs and stir to incorporate. Add the grated beets and stir to combine.

To make the cashew cheese, put the white beans, basil, garlic powder and sea salt in a medium-sized bowl and mash with a potato masher or large fork until combined. Put the cashews and ⅓ cup water in a blender and process until smooth, adding a bit more water if needed, until the cashews look like thick whipped cream. Add the cashew mixture to the white beans and mash to achieve a "ricotta cheese-like" consistency.

Spread ⅔ cup marinara sauce evenly in the bottom of a 9- x 12-inch or similarly sized casserole dish. Arrange one-third of the squash "noodles" over the sauce. Spread the beet mixture over the squash in an even layer. Spread ⅔ cup of the marinara sauce over the beet mixture. Arrange one-third of the squash "noodles" over the beet mixture. Spread the cashew cheese over the squash in an even layer.

Cut the remaining squash "lasagna noodles" into strips by slicing them lengthwise into long strips. Arrange the squash strips in a criss-cross pattern over the cashew

cheese layer (see photo, above). Spoon about 1 heaping tablespoon of marinara sauce in between the squash strips. Sprinkle 2 tablespoons chopped basil over the top.

Tent with foil and bake 45 to 50 minutes or until bubbling and squash is soft. Uncover and bake 5 to 7 minutes more to brown the top slightly. Let cool for 15 minutes before cutting into squares. Garnish with more fresh chopped basil and serve.

This gluten-free "noodle" dish showcases carrots in place of pasta. It's reminiscent of a New York-style, Chinese restaurant favorite and it makes a quick, delicious first course, side dish or light luncheon entrée.

Peanut-y CARROT "NOODLES"

MAKES 2 TO 4 SERVINGS

CARROT "NOODLES"

4 to 6 medium (or 3 to 4 large) **carrots, peeled**

PEANUT SAUCE

4 heaping tablespoons creamy peanut butter (see note)

2 tablespoons maple syrup

2 teaspoons gluten-free tamari

3 to 6 tablespoons water, plus more as needed

Dash cayenne pepper

TOPPINGS

1 scallion (white and green parts) **thinly sliced, for garnish**

1 small lime, cut in wedges (optional)

Cut the carrots into thin "noodles" using a vegetable peeler spiralizer (or regular spiralizer). Fit a steamer basket into a medium-sized sauce pan with a tight-fitting lid. Add 2 to 3 inches of water, and then add the carrots. Cover and bring to a boil. Steam the carrots for 2 to 3 minutes or until they are *al dente*.

Meanwhile, to make the sauce, put the peanut butter, maple syrup, tamari, 3 tablespoons of water and a dash of cayenne pepper into a small bowl and briskly whisk until combined. Add more water, 1 tablespoon at a time, to achieve desired consistency. Transfer the warm carrots to a medium-sized bowl and pour the sauce over the carrot "noodles." Gently toss using tongs or a large fork until the carrots are thoroughly coated with the peanut sauce. Serve warm or cover and refrigerate for 2 hours and serve cold. To serve, divide the carrot "noodles" into two to four pretty bowls. Top each bowl of carrot "noodles" with some scallions, with optional lime wedge on the side.

CHEF'S NOTE: *If you prefer, you may use cashew, almond or sunflower seed butter in place of peanut butter.*

GLUTEN-FREE

Quick and jazzylicious! This satisfying soup features thinly sliced cabbage that stands in perfectly for noodles! This dish makes a lovely luncheon entrée but serves equally well as a first course for a festive meal.

Sweet Potato SOUP WITH CABBAGE "NOODLES"

MAKES 3 TO 4 SERVINGS

- 2 very large sweet potatoes, peeled and cubed
- 3 celery stalks, with leaves, sliced
- 4 to 5 cups thinly sliced green cabbage "noodles" (see note)
- 6 to 7 cups vegetable broth, plus more as needed
- ½ cup chopped fresh parsley
- Sea salt, to taste (optional)

Put the sweet potatoes, celery, cabbage and vegetable broth in a medium-sized soup pot. Add more broth if needed to cover the vegetables. Cover and bring to a boil over medium heat. Once boiling, decrease the heat to medium-low and cook for 20 minutes. Add the parsley and cook for 5 to 10 minutes more, or until the vegetables are soft. Taste and add some sea salt, if desired. Serve hot.

CHEF'S NOTE: *To make the cabbage "noodles," cut a head of cabbage in half or in quarters. Cut out the core and then slice across the cabbage to make long "noodle-like" strands.*

Okay I'll admit it. I *really* dislike washing dishes, especially pots and pans. Whenever I can prepare a meal that cooks up in one big pan, pot or casserole, I'm in! So whether you're seeking easy-to-prepare meals or, like me, want to cut down on kitchen clean up tasks, these flavorful recipes are for you! From veggie stews to satisfying casseroles to hearty pasta dishes, here's a variety of one-pot meals to make your life better. (You're welcome.)

CHAPTER TWELVE

One-Pot Suppers

Lentil, Brown Rice and Carrot Stew, *page 197*

GLUTEN-FREE

This variation on a French Provençal dish is made easy by baking it in the oven—no sautéing required! It's a great choice for a weeknight supper.

Ratatouille BAKE

MAKES 4 SERVINGS

- **3½ cups cubed Japanese or baby Italian eggplant** (cut into 1 to 1½-inch slices, see note)
- **3 cups chopped zucchini** (1 to 1½-inch cubes)
- **2½ cups seeded and sliced red** (or orange) **mini sweet peppers or sweet bell peppers**
- **½ large sweet onion, diced**
- **1 can** (14 to 16 ounces) **diced tomatoes, with juice**
- **¼ cup water**
- **2 tablespoons extra-virgin olive oil**
- **1 tablespoon gluten-free tamari**
- **1 teaspoon Italian seasoning blend**
- **½ teaspoon garlic powder**
- **⅛ teaspoon crushed red pepper**
- **⅛ teaspoon sea salt, plus more to taste**

Preheat the oven to 400 degrees F. Put all of the ingredients into a large bowl and stir to combine. Transfer to a large casserole dish with tight fitting lid. Cover and bake for 1 hour or until veggies are soft and casserole is bubbling (see note). Let cool 10 minutes. Taste and add more sea salt to taste. Spoon into shallow bowls and serve.

CHEF'S NOTE: *I suggest setting the casserole dish on a baking pan while it cooks, in case any of the juices spill over while baking, to keep the oven clean!*

CHEF'S NOTE: *I like to use either a Japanese (Asian eggplant) or baby Italian eggplant in this recipe. Both varieties are thinner, with a more delicate skin than regular, larger eggplants, and the flesh is sweeter. If you are using a large eggplant, scoop out the brown seeds with a grapefruit spoon or sturdy teaspoon before cutting it into 1- to 1½-inch cubes.*

GLUTEN-FREE

My husband loves Chinese-style fried rice, so seeing his face light up when I served him this yummy, low-fat version was a treat. Bonus: it's super easy to prepare, too.

OVEN "Fried Rice" CASSEROLE

MAKES 3 TO 4 SERVINGS

- 2½ cups bite-sized broccoli florets
- 2 cups *cooked* brown basmati rice
- 1½ cups firmly packed, sliced baby bok choy
- 1¼ cups shredded carrots (peeling is optional)
- 1¼ cups vegetable broth
- ¾ cup roasted and salted cashews
- 3 small cloves garlic, minced
- 1 tablespoon minced fresh ginger
- 1 teaspoon gluten-free tamari

Preheat the oven to 400 degrees F. Put all of the ingredients in a large bowl and stir with a large spoon to combine. Transfer to a 9- x 11-inch or similarly sized casserole. Cover and bake for 30 to 40 minutes or until the vegetables are soft and the casserole is heated through. Serve hot.

GLUTEN-FREE

This sensational stew has many ingredients, but it is actually very easy to prepare in one big pot, and has a real kick to it, with a bit of an Indian flair.

Spicy CHICKPEA AND POTATO STEW

MAKES 6 SERVINGS

½ large red onion, diced

1 cup water, plus more as needed

1 teaspoon gluten-free tamari

3 cups quartered baby red potatoes (peeling is optional)

1½ cups sliced carrots (peeling is optional)

2 cups chopped fresh tomatoes

1 large clove garlic, minced

1 teaspoon ground cumin

½ teaspoon ground turmeric

½ teaspoon chili powder

½ teaspoon dried cilantro

¼ teaspoon sea salt, plus more as needed

⅛ teaspoon freshly ground black pepper, plus more as needed

1 can (15 to 16 ounces) chickpeas (garbanzo beans), drained and rinsed

2 cups bite-sized cauliflower florets

1½ cups peeled and diced sweet potatoes

1 cup green beans, trimmed and cut into 1½-inch pieces

Put the onion, water and tamari into a large soup pot. Cover and cook over medium heat for 2 minutes, stirring occasionally. Decrease the heat to medium-low. Add the red potatoes, carrots and tomatoes. Cover and cook, stirring occasionally, for 5 minutes. Add the garlic, cumin, turmeric, chili powder, cilantro, sea salt and black pepper and bring to a simmer. Cover and cook for 2 minutes. Add the chickpeas, cauliflower, sweet potatoes and green beans. Add a bit more water, if needed, to cover the vegetables by about ½-inch. Cover and simmer for 30 to 35 minutes, stirring occasionally, until the veggies are soft and the stew has thickened, adding more water as needed if the stew becomes dry. Taste and add more salt and pepper, if desired. Serve warm.

See photo of this recipe on page 196.

Spicy Chickpea and Potato Stew *(page 195), above*

Lentil, Brown Rice and Carrot Stew *(page 197), below*

GLUTEN-FREE

This delightfully fragrant and satisfying stew makes a great weeknight offering, and it makes impressive fare for company, too. The garlic adds real pizzazz without overwhelming the other ingredients. Make this one-dish wonder the star of your menu on a chilly late summer evening or cold autumn night.

LENTIL, BROWN RICE AND CARROT *Stew*

MAKES 6 TO 8 SERVINGS

- **4½ cups chopped zucchini** (cut into 1- to 1½-inch cubes)
- **2 cups chopped fresh tomatoes**
- **1⅔ cups sliced carrots** (peeling is optional)
- **1 cup *uncooked* long-grain or short-grain brown rice, rinsed**
- **1 cup *uncooked* green lentils, sorted, cleaned and rinsed** (see note, page 132)
- **1 small sweet onion, chopped**
- **2 tablespoons thinly sliced fresh garlic**
- **2 large vegan gluten-free bouillon cubes, crumbled**
- **1½ teaspoons gluten-free tamari**
- **10 cups water, plus more as needed**
- **3 cups lightly packed, de-stemmed, thinly sliced kale**
- **¼ cup chopped fresh basil**
- **Sea salt, to taste**
- **Freshly ground black pepper, to taste**

Put the zucchini, tomatoes, carrots, rice, lentils, onion, garlic, crumbled bouillon cubes and tamari in a large soup pot. Pour in the water and stir to combine. Cover and cook over medium-low heat, stirring occasionally, for 40 minutes. Add the kale, cover and cook, stirring occasionally, for 15 minutes. Add more water if needed. Add the basil and cook for 5 to 10 minutes more, or until the lentils and rice are soft. Season with salt and pepper, to taste. Serve in deep soup bowls with green salad on the side, if desired.

This one-pot dish is brimming with flavor and nutrients, making a great entrée for a busy weeknight supper.

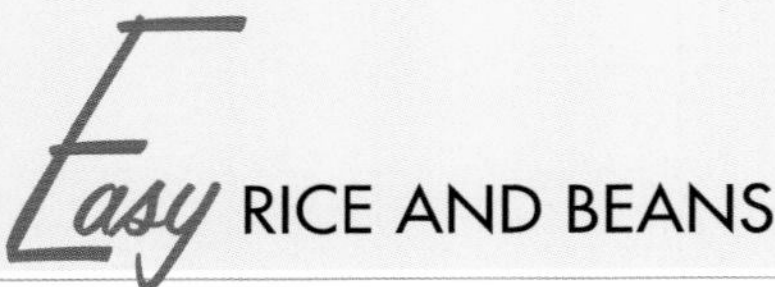

Easy RICE AND BEANS

MAKES 3 TO 4 SERVINGS

1 sweet onion, chopped
2 small cloves garlic, chopped
1 teaspoon dried cilantro
1 teaspoon gluten-free tamari
½ teaspoon ground cumin
½ teaspoon ground turmeric
Dash crushed red pepper flakes
1 tablespoon extra-virgin olive oil
2¼ cups vegetable broth
1 can (15 to 16 ounces) black beans, drained and rinsed
1 cup *uncooked* brown basmati rice, rinsed

Put the onion, garlic, cilantro, tamari, cumin, turmeric, crushed red pepper and olive oil into a medium-sized saucepan. Cover and cook over medium heat for about 8 minutes until the onion is soft, stirring occasionally. Stir in the broth, beans and rice and bring to a boil. Decrease the heat to medium-low, cover and simmer for 45 to 50 minutes or until the rice is soft but not mushy. Take the pan off the heat and let stand for 5 to 10 minutes. Fluff with a fork and serve.

JAZZY TIP: *Turmeric, a member of the ginger family, is a great spice to add to your vegan recipe repertoire. Its stunning yellow-orange color enhances the visual appeal of many dishes, and the unique flavor of turmeric imparts depth. Turmeric is touted as having numerous health benefits and has long been used in both Chinese and Ayurvedic medicine. Try adding turmeric to rice and beans, tofu scramble, sautéed veggies or a wide variety of recipes made with tofu, tempeh, grains or vegetables.*

GLUTEN-FREE OPTION

This zingy chili has a jazzy kick to it with the addition of smoked paprika and a bit of cayenne pepper. It's so easy to prepare and even easier to eat!

SIMPLY DELICIOUS Chili

MAKES 8 SERVINGS

- 1 large sweet onion, chopped
- 1 tablespoon extra-virgin olive oil, divided
- 1 tablespoon gluten-free tamari, divided
- 1 teaspoon chili powder
- ½ teaspoon smoked paprika
- ⅛ teaspoon cayenne pepper
- 1 large orange or red sweet bell pepper, seeded and chopped
- ⅓ cup plus 2 tablespoons water, plus more as needed
- 1 large can (24 to 28 ounces) fire-roasted crushed tomatoes
- 2 cans (14 to 16 ounces each) black beans, drained and rinsed
- 1 can (14 to 16 ounces) kidney beans, drained and rinsed
- 1 tablespoon vegan brown sugar, or your preferred dry sweetener
- 1 package (8 ounces) traditional style seitan, sliced (see note for gluten-free option)

Put the onion, ½ tablespoon olive oil, ½ tablespoon tamari, chili powder, smoked paprika and cayenne into a large soup pot and cook over medium heat for 3 to 4 minutes until the onion becomes almost translucent. Add the bell pepper and 2 tablespoons of water and cook for 5 to 10 minutes, stirring often, until onion and pepper are slightly golden, adding a bit more water as needed if the pan becomes dry.

Decrease the heat to medium-low. Add the tomatoes, ⅓ cup water, ½ tablespoon olive oil, ½ tablespoon tamari, black beans, kidney beans and sugar. Cover and cook for 30 minutes, stirring occasionally. Add the seitan, cover and cook, stirring occasionally, for 30 minutes more, or until the chili is nice and thick. Serve in soup bowls with green salad on the side, if desired.

CHEF'S NOTE: *To make this dish gluten free, omit the seitan and add an additional 8 ounces of kidney beans when you are adding the beans to the pot. Proceed with recipe as directed.*

GLUTEN-FREE OPTION

So simple but oh so satisfying, this one-pot pasta makes great use of fresh spring asparagus. The entire dish whips up in less than 20 minutes, making this an ideal solution for a delicious, home cooked weeknight meal.

Penne WITH ASPARAGUS AND HERBED "BUTTER" SAUCE

MAKES 4 TO 6 SERVINGS

1 pound *uncooked* penne pasta (use gluten-free variety for a gluten-free option)

4½ cups fresh asparagus, trimmed and cut in 1½ to 2-inch lengths

3 tablespoons vegan buttery spread, plus more as needed

1 teaspoon dried parsley, or 1 tablespoon chopped fresh parsley

1 teaspoon dried basil, or 1 tablespoon chopped fresh basil

¼ teaspoon dried marjoram

¼ teaspoon garlic powder

¼ teaspoon sea salt, plus more as needed

⅛ teaspoon ground turmeric (optional)

Freshly ground black pepper, to taste

Bring a large pot of salted water to a boil over medium-high heat. Stir in the penne. Decrease the heat to medium-low and cook, stirring occasionally, for 8 minutes. Add the asparagus, stir and cook for 3 to 4 minutes or until the penne is cooked *al dente* and the asparagus is crisp tender.

Meanwhile, put the vegan buttery spread, parsley, basil, marjoram, garlic powder, sea salt and optional turmeric into a bowl large enough to also accommodate the penne and the asparagus, and whip vigorously with a fork until well combined.

Drain the penne and asparagus, and while they are still piping hot, pour them over the buttery herb mixture. Toss gently until thoroughly combined. Season with more salt and freshly ground pepper, to taste, and toss again. If the pasta seems slightly dry, add a bit more vegan buttery spread, to taste. Serve immediately.

Photo courtesy of Annie Olivero. Learn more about Annie on page 296.

This nutritious and delicious pasta dish, which can be prepared in under 20 minutes, is an ideal one-pot meal. The optional wheat germ stands in well for parmesan cheese. It also helps hold the ingredients together and adds texture and flavor.

Quick Penne WITH BROCCOLI AND SUN-DRIED TOMATOES

MAKES 4 TO 6 SERVINGS

1 pound *uncooked* whole-grain or gluten-free penne (or fusilli) pasta

1 large bunch broccoli, cut into bite-size florets

1 jar (8 ounces) oil-packed sun-dried tomatoes, drained and chopped

2 tablespoons extra-virgin olive oil, divided, plus more as needed

12 large leaves fresh basil, very thinly sliced, or 2 teaspoons dried basil

¼ teaspoon garlic powder

¼ cup toasted wheat germ (optional, omit for gluten-free option)

Sea salt, to taste

Freshly ground black pepper, to taste

Bring a large pot of salted water to a boil over medium-high heat. Stir in the penne. Decrease the heat to medium-low and cook, stirring occasionally, until the penne is almost tender. Add the broccoli and cook, stirring occasionally, for 3 to 4 minutes or until the penne is cooked *al dente* and the broccoli is crisp tender.

Meanwhile, put the sun-dried tomatoes, 1 tablespoon of oil, basil and garlic powder in a bowl large enough to also accommodate the penne and broccoli and stir until well combined.

Drain the penne and broccoli, and while they are still piping hot, pour them over the tomato mixture. Add the optional wheat germ and toss gently until thoroughly combined. Add 1 more tablespoon olive oil, plus more if desired. Season with salt and pepper to taste and toss again. Serve immediately.

GLUTEN-FREE OPTION

Reminiscent of my mom's tasty spaghetti pie, this tasty weeknight offering makes great use of leftover pasta. This recipe does use a pot *and* a casserole dish, but it's so simple to assemble that I decided to include it here. Plus, the spinach is hidden in the layers, making it a kid friendly, hearty weeknight meal.

Spaghetti CASSEROLE

MAKES 4 SERVINGS

1 medium sweet onion, diced

1 tablespoon extra-virgin olive oil

4 tablespoons water, plus more as needed

1 teaspoon gluten-free tamari

8 ounces white button mushrooms, sliced

1 teaspoon Italian seasoning blend

¼ teaspoon crushed red pepper (use ⅛ teaspoon for less heat or omit for the kiddos)

1 jar (24 to 26 ounces) **vegan marinara sauce, divided**

8 ounces *cooked* whole-grain or gluten-free spaghetti (I use *leftover* spaghetti!)

4 to 5 ounces baby spinach

⅔ cup shredded vegan mozzarella-style cheese (see note)

Put the onion, olive oil, 2 tablespoons water and tamari in a large skillet. Cover and cook over medium heat for 5 minutes. Add the mushrooms, Italian seasoning, crushed red pepper and 2 more tablespoons water. Cover and cook over medium heat, stirring occasionally, for 5 minutes. Add more water, 1 tablespoon at a time, if the pan becomes dry (see note).

Preheat the oven to 400 degrees F. In a 9- x 12-inch or similarly sized casserole, spread 1 cup of the marinara sauce in an even layer. Arrange the cooked spaghetti in an even layer over the marinara sauce. Top with ⅓ cup of the marinara sauce. Spread the mushroom and onion mixture in an even layer over the marinara sauce. Add the baby spinach and press down. Spread the remaining marinara sauce (about 1¼ cups) over the top of the casserole. Tent with foil and bake for 40 minutes. Uncover and top with vegan cheese. Bake uncovered for 7 to 10 minutes or until vegan cheese is melted and casserole is bubbling. Put the dish on a wire rack and let cool for 10 minutes before serving.

CHEF'S NOTE: *If you are cooking gluten free, make certain to purchase certified gluten-free vegan cheese, available in most supermarkets.*

CHEF'S NOTE: *The mushroom/onion mixture can be made a day in advance of baking this recipe. Store tightly covered in the refrigerator until using.*

GLUTEN-FREE

This simple but flavorful blend of cauliflower and marinara sauce works beautifully as a delicious entrée. To round out the meal, serve this dish over *cooked* quinoa or brown rice, if desired.

CAULIFLOWER-Marinara Bake

MAKES 4 SERVINGS

- 1 medium head cauliflower, cut into bite-size florets
- 12 to 14 ounces vegan marinara sauce
- ½ cup water, plus more as needed
- 2 teaspoons extra-virgin olive oil
- 2 teaspoons Italian seasoning blend
- ¼ teaspoon crushed red pepper

Preheat the oven to 375 degrees F. Put all of the ingredients into a large bowl and stir, using a large spoon, until combined (see note). Transfer the cauliflower mixture to a medium-sized casserole, cover and bake for 45 to 50 minutes or until the cauliflower is soft and the marinara sauce is bubbling. Serve warm.

CHEF'S NOTE: *Two cups of cauliflower florets has about 4 grams of protein, but if you would like to add more protein to this dish, simply add 1 can (14 to 16 ounces) of black beans, white beans or chickpeas (garbanzo beans) when stirring together all of the other ingredients.*

I'm often asked: "What can I serve as the star of my menu, especially when I'm preparing a meal for family or company?" Good question! My solution is to feature main dishes that highlight robust veggies (such as portobello mushrooms, winter squash, zucchini, cauliflower or even sweet bell peppers), meaty tasting protein substitutes (like tofu, seitan, tempeh, beans and lentils) and/or nuts and seeds (like walnuts, almonds, cashews, pecans and sunflower seeds). This chapter includes dishes that are simple to prepare for weeknight suppers, plus festive entrées you'll be proud to serve at fun family get-togethers or formal dinner parties. With these *jazzilicious* meals, everyone will be happy and *no one will miss the meat.*

Greek-*ish* Pizza, *page 219*

CHAPTER THIRTEEN

Meal Stars

GLUTEN-FREE OPTION

This tempting, hearty entrée is especially well-suited to wintertime, and the festive presentation will grace the table at any holiday celebration. Choose the color of peppers accordingly: orange and yellow for Thanksgiving, red and green for Christmas or red for Valentine's Day. The quinoa has a light, nutty flavor that perfectly complements the black beans.

Fancy STUFFED PEPPERS with Quinoa and Black Beans

MAKES 6 SERVINGS

1 cup *uncooked* quinoa, rinsed thoroughly

2 cups vegetable broth

6 medium sweet bell peppers, any color or a combination of colors

1 tablespoon extra-virgin olive oil

⅔ jar (18 to 20 ounces) vegan marinara sauce, divided, plus more as needed

1 can (15 to 16 ounces) black beans, drained and rinsed

6 ounces cremini or white button mushrooms, chopped

1 medium sweet onion, chopped

¼ cup toasted wheat germ, plus more as needed (see note for gluten-free option)

2 cloves garlic, chopped

1 teaspoon dried basil

CHEF'S NOTE: *Depending upon the size of your peppers, you may have leftover quinoa stuffing. If so, put it in a small, covered casserole and bake along with the peppers.*

CHEF'S NOTE: *For gluten-free option, use gluten-free oat bran in place of the wheat germ.*

Put the quinoa and broth in a medium-sized saucepan and bring to a boil over medium-high heat. Decrease the heat to medium-low, cover and simmer for 15 to 17 minutes or until the water is absorbed and the quinoa is soft. Let cool for 15 minutes. Transfer to a bowl, cover and refrigerate for 2 to 24 hours.

When ready to assemble the peppers, preheat the oven to 400 degrees F. Slice off the top ½- to ¾-inch from each pepper and reserve. (These tops will be used to "cap" the peppers later.) Seed the peppers. Put the oil and ½ cup marinara in a small bowl and stir to combine. Spread the marinara mixture over the bottom of a deep casserole dish large enough to hold all the peppers snugly so they remain upright during baking.

Put the cooked quinoa, beans, mushrooms, onion, wheat germ or gluten-free oat bran, garlic, basil and 1 cup marinara sauce into a large bowl and stir until well combined, adding more marinara sauce, ¼ cup at a time, until the mixture is very moist but not soupy.

Spoon one-sixth of the quinoa mixture into each pepper, mounding it above the top. Spoon 1 tablespoon of marinara sauce over each pepper, and then top with the reserved pepper tops. (Stuffing will peek out; see note.) Arrange the peppers upright in the casserole. Cover and bake for 40 to 55 minutes or until the sauce is bubbly and the peppers are tender. Let cool for 15 minutes. Put any sauce that has accumulated at the bottom of the casserole in a gravy boat to pass at the table. Serve with *Sweet and Savory Kale* (page 238, see photo on opposite page) on the side, if desired.

GLUTEN-FREE OPTION

One evening I was hosting a casual dinner for close friends. I wanted to impress, but being that it was a weeknight, I was really short on prep time. I came up with this marvelous, eight-ingredient mushroom recipe that tastes great and presents well, too!

QUICK *Stuffed Portobello* MUSHROOMS

MAKES 4 TO 6 SERVINGS

6 medium portobello mushrooms, washed with stems removed

1 tablespoon plus 1½ teaspoons extra-virgin olive oil, divided, plus more as needed

1 tablespoon gluten-free tamari

5 to 6 slices vegan whole-grain or gluten-free bread, torn in several pieces

1 tablespoon all-purpose seasoning

½ teaspoon sea salt, plus more as needed

¾ cup chopped pecans

2 cups firmly packed baby spinach, finely chopped

Preheat the oven to 400 degrees F. Line a large, rimmed baking pan with unbleached parchment paper. Arrange the mushrooms on the lined pan, gill side up. Spoon ¼ teaspoon olive oil and ½ teaspoon tamari over the gills of each mushroom.

Put the bread, all-purpose seasoning and salt in a blender or food processor and process into coarse crumbs. Transfer to a large bowl. Put the pecans in a blender and process until coarsely ground. Transfer the pecans to the bowl with the bread crumbs. Add the baby spinach and 1 tablespoon olive oil and stir to combine, adding more olive oil if the crumbs are still dry. Divide the bread crumb mixture evenly among the portobello mushrooms, mounding about ½ cup of the mixture in each (using an ice-cream scoop works well). Press the mixture firmly in place so it will adhere to the mushrooms while baking.

Tent the mushrooms with foil and bake for 40 to 50 minutes. Remove the foil and bake uncovered for 5 to 10 minutes longer, or until the topping is crisp and the mushrooms are tender. Serve immediately with *Rosemary Smashed Potatoes* (page 240) on the side.

GLUTEN-FREE

These delicious "cutlets" are a breeze to prepare and a delight to serve. The flavorful sauce transforms cauliflowers from a notoriously "bland" veggie into a delicious cruciferous entrée.

BBQ CAULIFLOWER CUTLETS

MAKES 4 SERVINGS

BBQ SAUCE

- 6 tablespoons ketchup
- 1½ tablespoons maple syrup
- 1 tablespoon spicy brown or Dijon mustard
- ¼ teaspoon garlic powder
- ¼ teaspoon smoked paprika
- 1⁄16 teaspoon cayenne pepper

CUTLETS

- 2 medium heads of cauliflower
- 6 teaspoons extra-virgin olive oil, divided
- ¼ teaspoon smoked paprika

To make the BBQ sauce, put the ketchup, maple syrup, mustard, garlic powder, smoked paprika and cayenne pepper in a small bowl and stir to combine.

Preheat the oven to 375 degrees F. Line a medium-sized, rimmed baking pan with unbleached parchment paper. Trim about 2-inches off the two opposite sides of each cauliflower head and set aside for another use. Carefully cut each cauliflower head into two ¾- to 1-inch thick "cutlets," as if slicing a loaf of bread. Arrange the cutlets in a single layer on the prepared baking sheet.

Lightly coat the parchment paper with 2 teaspoons olive oil. Arrange the cauliflower cutlets in a single layer on the parchment paper. Brush each cutlet with 1 teaspoon olive oil and sprinkle with 1⁄16 teaspoon of smoked paprika. Tent with foil and bake for 20 to 25 minutes or until the cauliflower begins to soften. Increase the oven to 425 degrees F. Put the pan on a wire rack and *carefully* remove the foil. (Cutlets will be steaming hot!) Spread 1 tablespoon of the BBQ sauce evenly over the top of each cutlet. Bake for 10 to 12 minutes. Remove the pan from the oven and add another ½ to 1 tablespoon of BBQ sauce to each cauliflower cutlet. Bake for 6 to 12 minutes more, or until the edges of the cauliflower cutlets are golden and the sauce is bubbling hot. Transfer the pan to a wire rack and let cool 5 minutes. Serve with *Sneaky Spinach Mash-Up* (page 239) on the side.

GLUTEN-FREE OPTION

My mom often made sukiyaki when I was a girl and I loved it! Recently, she sent me the recipe so I could "veganize" it, and I couldn't be more pleased with the results. I hope you will love it too!

VEGAN Sukiyaki

MAKES 4 SERVINGS

1 large sweet onion, sliced

2 tablespoons extra-virgin olive oil, divided

2 tablespoons plus 2 teaspoons gluten-free tamari, divided

8 ounces cremini or white button mushrooms, sliced

3 very large stalks celery, thinly sliced

1 cup plus 2 tablespoons vegetable broth, divided

1 block (14 to 16 ounces) **extra-firm tofu, pressed 1 to 3 hours** (see note, page 220) **and cut into cubes** (see note)

8 ounces seitan, thinly sliced (see note for gluten-free option)

¾ large head napa cabbage, cut into thin strips

2 to 4 heads baby bok choy, cut in half lengthwise

3 tablespoons maple syrup

Put the onion, 1 tablespoon olive oil, and 1 teaspoon tamari into a 12- to 14-inch wide large, deep skillet and cook over medium heat, stirring occasionally, for 3 minutes. Add the mushrooms, celery, 3 tablespoons broth and 1 more teaspoon tamari. Cover and cook over medium heat for 7 minutes, stirring occasionally. Transfer the onion/celery mixture to a plate and loosely cover to keep warm.

Put the tofu, seitan, 1 tablespoon olive oil and 2 tablespoons broth into the skillet and cook for 5 to 6 minutes, turning the tofu and seitan after 3 minutes. Push the tofu and seitan to the side of the skillet. Add the napa cabbage into a separate corner of the skillet, pushing the cabbage down to help compress it so it will *almost* fit in the skillet. Add the onion/celery mixture, pushing it into a separate corner of the skillet. Add the bok choy to a separate section of the skillet. Add the remaining broth. Put 2 tablespoons tamari and the maple syrup into a small bowl and briskly whisk to combine. Pour the tamari/maple mixture over all of the ingredients in the skillet. Decrease the heat to medium-low. Press the cover down over the ingredients (the cabbage will make it *almost* overflowing, but it will *really* cook down!) and cook for 10 to 11 minutes or until the veggies are tender (see photo on this page). Serve each person one-quarter of the sukiyaki with *Basmati Rice with Cashews and Scallions* (page 249) on the side.

CHEF'S NOTE: *If you are cooking gluten free, replace the seitan with an additional ½ to ¾ block (8 to 12 ounces) of pressed and cubed tofu. Make certain to purchase certified gluten-free tofu, available in most supermarkets.*

This lovely little loaf is easy to assemble, making a perfect, plant-powered main entrée for a festive supper.

Nutty ZUCCHINI LOAF

MAKES 4 TO 6 SERVINGS

- 3 large slices vegan whole-grain or gluten-free bread
- ¾ cup gluten-free, quick cooking rolled oats
- ½ cup chopped raw cashews
- ½ cup chopped walnuts
- ¼ cup roasted and salted sunflower seeds
- 1⅓ cups lightly packed, shredded zucchini (about 1 medium)
- 1 teaspoon all-purpose seasoning
- ½ teaspoon sea salt
- ½ teaspoon smoked paprika
- ¼ teaspoon garlic powder
- 2 tablespoons extra-virgin olive oil, plus more as needed

Line an 8- x 4-inch loaf pan with unbleached parchment paper, leaving a 2½-inch overhang on the two lengthwise sides of the pan to make paper "wings." Put the whole-grain bread into a blender and process into coarse crumbs. Transfer the bread crumbs to a large bowl. Add the oats to the bread crumbs. Put the cashews, walnuts and sunflower seeds into the blender and process into coarse crumbs. Add the nut mixture to the bread crumb/oat mixture. Stir with a large spoon to combine.

Add the zucchini, all-purpose seasoning, sea salt, smoked paprika and garlic powder and stir to combine. Drizzle the olive oil over the mixture and stir until evenly coated with olive oil. Add 1 more tablespoon olive oil if the mixture still seems dry. Spoon the loaf mixture into the prepared pan and smooth the top of the loaf with a spatula. Fold the paper "wings" over the top of the loaf and gently press down with your hands (see photo). This will to help to hold the loaf together while it bakes. Refrigerate the loaf for 1 to 4 hours to help it firm up before baking.

When you're ready to bake the loaf, preheat the oven to 375 degrees F. Bake the loaf for 30 minutes. Put the pan on a wire rack and carefully peel back the parchment paper "wings" that are covering the top of the loaf. Bake uncovered for an additional 15 to 25 minutes or until the loaf is firm to the touch and golden brown around the edges.

Transfer the pan to a wire rack and let cool for 10 to 15 minutes to allow it to firm up slightly. Using the paper "wings," lift the loaf out of the pan and put it on a cutting board. Carefully peel off the parchment paper. Carefully cut the loaf into 6 to 8 slices, using a serrated bread knife and wiping the knife clean after cutting each slice (loaf will be *soft*). Serve the loaf, smothered in *Yummiest Mushroom-Onion Gravy* (page 92) with *Tiny Potatoes with Spicy Mustard Sauce* (page 243) on the side, if desired.

This incredibly colorful and appetizing pizza is a real winner with vegans and omnivores alike. Topped with tangy olives, roasted sweet peppers, baby spinach and an authentic tasting homemade vegan "feta," this plant-powered twist on pizza will take you and your family on a trip to the Mediterranean in your own kitchen!

GREEK-*ISH* Pizza

MAKES 1 10-INCH PIZZA

3 teaspoons extra-virgin olive oil, divided

½ small clove garlic, minced

¼ teaspoon sea salt, divided

1 10 to 11-inch store-bought, pre-made vegan pizza crust or Italian-style flatbread crust

1½ cups baby spinach, chopped

6 pitted Kalamata olives, cut in half

6 slices (jarred) roasted red sweet bell pepper

¼ cup *Best Vegan "Feta"* (page 84)

Several fresh basil leaves, torn into pieces

Preheat the oven to 425 degrees F. Put the crust on a pizza pan or large, rimmed baking pan. Put 2 teaspoons olive oil, minced garlic and ⅛ teaspoon sea salt into a small bowl and stir with a spoon to combine. Spread the olive oil mixture evenly over the crust, leaving a 1-inch rim around the edge of crust.

Put the baby spinach in a bowl and toss it with 1 teaspoon of olive oil and ⅛ teaspoon salt. Arrange the spinach mixture over the olive oil/garlic mixture on the crust.

Arrange the Kalamata olives, roasted red peppers and feta in a pleasing pattern over the top of the spinach. Bake for 8 to 15 minutes or until the crust is golden and the toppings are hot. Transfer to a wire rack and let cool for 5 to 7 minutes. Sprinkle fresh basil over the top of the pizza, slice and serve.

GLUTEN-FREE

This recipe comes in handy when you need a filling protein component for a meal. The tofu can be served warm alongside a baked potato and sautéed greens for supper, or chilled and used in dishes like *Jazzy Salad Niçoise* (page 100).

Maple BAKED TOFU

MAKES 3 TO 4 SERVINGS

1 block (14 to 16 ounces) **extra-firm regular tofu, drained and pressed** (see notes)

1½ tablespoons gluten-free tamari (use 2 tablespoons for a saltier baked tofu)

1 tablespoon water

1 tablespoon extra-virgin olive oil

1 tablespoon maple syrup (use 2 tablespoons for a sweeter baked tofu)

Slice the pressed tofu into 9 to 12 equal sized "cutlets." Line an 8-inch square, rimmed baking pan with unbleached parchment paper. Arrange the tofu cutlets in a snug, even layer in the prepared pan. Put the tamari, water, olive oil and maple syrup into a small bowl and briskly whisk to combine. Pour over the tofu. Tent with foil and refrigerate 30 minutes to 1 hour, to allow the tofu to marinate.

Preheat the oven to 375 degrees F. Bake the tofu (covered) for 25 minutes. Put the pan on a wire rack and carefully remove the foil. Flip the tofu and bake uncovered for 30 to 45 minutes more (depending upon the thickness of your cutlets), or until golden brown on both sides. Transfer the pan to a wire rack and let cool for 5 minutes before serving. Tightly covered and stored in the refrigerator, baked tofu will keep for up to 4 days.

CHEF'S NOTE: *If you are cooking gluten free, make certain to purchase certified gluten-free tofu, available in most supermarkets.*

CHEF'S NOTE: *For some tofu recipes requiring baking or sautéing, it is important to press the excess liquid out of the tofu first so that your recipe does not become too watery. If you cook with tofu often, I highly recommend purchasing a tofu press. However, if you do not own a tofu press, you may press the tofu by putting the block of tofu on a rimmed dinner plate that has been covered in a layer of paper towels or clean kitchen towel. Put another layer of towels on top of the tofu. Put another plate (or a small cutting board) on top of the paper towels and weigh it down with a heavy object like a few soup cans. Refrigerate. After 1 to 3 hours, drain the water that has been pressed out of the tofu. Your tofu is now ready for use in any recipe requiring pressed tofu.*

GLUTEN-FREE

These sassy "steaks" are smothered in a colorful sauce that's simple to make but full of robust flavor. Steaming the cauliflower first cuts down on baking time, making this a welcome weeknight entrée. Now you can make cauliflower the star of your meal!

CAULIFLOWER *Steaks* WITH SWEET PEPPER SAUCE

MAKES 4 TO 6 SERVINGS

2 medium/large heads of cauliflower
1 medium red onion, thinly sliced
1 medium sweet onion, thinly sliced
2 teaspoons Italian seasoning blend
1 tablespoon extra-virgin olive oil (optional)
1 teaspoon gluten-free tamari
¼ cup water, divided, plus more as needed
2 cups cremini or white button mushrooms, thinly sliced
2 red or orange sweet bell peppers, seeded and thinly sliced
1 green bell pepper, seeded and thinly sliced
2 cups prepared vegan marinara sauce

Preheat the oven to 375 degrees F. Trim about 2-inches off the two opposite sides of each cauliflower head and set aside for another use. Steam the trimmed cauliflower heads for 6 to 10 minutes or until *just* crisp tender. Cool for 20 minutes. Carefully cut each of the steamed cauliflower heads into two to three ¾- to 1-inch thick "cutlets," as if slicing a loaf of bread.

Meanwhile, put the onions, Italian seasoning, optional olive oil, tamari and 2 tablespoons water in a large skillet. Cover and cook over medium heat for 5 minutes, adding more water, 1 tablespoon at a time, as needed to prevent sticking. Add the mushrooms and cook for 5 minutes. Add the peppers and continue to cook for 5 minutes. Decrease the heat to medium-low and stir in 1 cup of the marinara. Cover and simmer for 6 minutes. Spread 1 cup marinara sauce over the bottom of a casserole dish that is large enough to accommodate the cauliflower steaks in a single layer. Put the cauliflower slices in the prepared casserole. Top each cauliflower slice with a generous amount of the onion and pepper sauce. Cover and bake for 12 to 16 minutes or until the cauliflower steaks are tender, but still firm. Uncover the casserole for the last 5 to 10 minutes of cooking time. Transfer the pan to a wire rack and let cool 5 minutes. Serve with *Sneaky Spinach Mash-Up* (page 239) or *Rosemary Smashed Potatoes* (page 240) and extra sauce on the side, if desired.

See photo of this recipe on page 222.

Cauliflower Steaks with Sweet Pepper Sauce *(page 221), above*

Spaghetti and Wheatballs *(page 223), below*

GLUTEN-FREE OPTION

This is one of my most famous *and* favorite recipes! These wheatballs have an authentic taste and texture, making it a foolproof crowd-pleaser for any family meal. This satisfying dish is easy enough to make for a weeknight meal, but fancy enough to serve when hosting a dinner party. Bonus: the wheatballs freeze well, too!

Spaghetti AND WHEATBALLS

MAKES 4 SERVINGS (12 TO 14 WHEATBALLS)

- 1⅓ cups lightly packed, freshly ground vegan whole-grain bread or gluten-free bread crumbs (see note)
- 1 teaspoon Italian seasoning blend
- ½ teaspoon garlic powder
- ⅛ teaspoon sea salt
- ½ cup chopped walnuts
- 2 cups chopped white button or cremini mushrooms
- ½ cup diced onion
- ¾ to 1 pound *uncooked* whole-grain or gluten-free spaghetti
- 3 cups prepared vegan marinara sauce or your own homemade sauce

CHEF'S NOTE: *To make fresh bread crumbs, put 3 to 4 slices of whole-grain or gluten-free bread in a blender and process into coarse crumbs.*

CHEF'S NOTE: *To make this recipe gluten free, use a vegan, gluten-free bread to make your bread crumbs. Keep in mind: without the gluten in the bread, the wheatballs may be softer and crumblier in texture, but they are still delicious!*

Preheat the oven to 350 degrees F. Line a medium-sized baking pan with unbleached parchment paper. Put the bread crumbs, Italian seasoning, garlic powder and salt in a large bowl. Put the walnuts in a blender and process into coarse crumbs. Add the walnuts to the bread crumbs and stir to combine. Put the mushrooms and onion in a blender and process to a chunky purée. Add the mushroom mixture to the walnut/bread crumb mixture and stir to combine. Scoop out about 1½ tablespoons of the mushroom mixture and roll it into a ball. Continue in this way with the remaining mushroom mixture to make 12 to 14 wheatballs. Arrange the rolled wheatballs on the lined baking pan. Bake for 25 to 30 minutes. Gently rotate each wheatball and bake for 12 to 20 minutes more, or until they are crisp and golden. (The wheatballs *will* be very *soft* at this point, so handle with care!)

Meanwhile, bring a large pot of salted water to a boil. Add the spaghetti and cook, stirring occasionally, until cooked *al dente*. Drain the spaghetti. While the spaghetti cooks, pour marinara sauce into a medium-sized saucepan and bring to a simmer over medium-low heat. Divide the spaghetti into four shallow pasta bowls, and gently top each bowl with 3 wheatballs. Ladle marinara sauce over the top of the spaghetti and sprinkle with *Cashew Parmesan Cheeze* (page 97), if desired. Serve immediately.

Pretty to look at and a delight to serve! These flavorful kebabs have an Asian flair and make a festive dinner entrée any day of the week.

Teriyaki SEITAN SKEWERS

MAKES 6 SERVINGS

SKEWERS

12 to 14 twelve-inch bamboo skewers, soaked in water for 15 to 20 minutes, to prevent them from burning while cooking

36 to 40 cherry tomatoes

1 bag (14 to 16 ounces) mini sweet peppers, seeded and sliced in half lengthwise

2 medium zucchini, cut into 36 slices

1 package (8 to 10 ounces) traditional-style seitan, cut into about 24 pieces

12 to 14 large cremini mushrooms, cut in half

TERIYAKI SAUCE

6 tablespoons maple syrup

4 tablespoons gluten-free tamari

3 tablespoons extra-virgin olive oil

½ teaspoon smoked paprika

½ teaspoon garlic powder

1⁄16 teaspoon cayenne pepper

Line a very large, rimmed baking sheet (about 20- x 14-inches) with unbleached parchment paper. Evenly divide and thread the veggies and seitan onto the prepared skewers. Arrange the kebabs in a single layer on the lined baking sheet.

To make the teriyaki sauce, put the maple syrup, tamari, olive oil, paprika, garlic powder and cayenne pepper in a small bowl and briskly whisk to combine. Brush the skewers with one-half of the teriyaki sauce. Cover loosely with unbleached parchment paper and refrigerate for 1 to 2 hours to marinate. Refrigerate the remaining teriyaki sauce, too.

When you are ready to cook the skewers, preheat the oven to 375 degrees F and bake the parchment covered skewers for 30 minutes. Put the pan on a wire rack and remove the parchment. Brush the remaining teriyaki sauce over the skewers. Bake uncovered, for 15 to 20 minutes more, or until golden brown. Serve 2 skewers per person with corn-on-the-cob on the side, if desired.

GLUTEN-FREE

Satisfying and hearty, these tasty kebabs are certainly guest-worthy and excellent to serve for a summer holiday meal *or* weeknight supper. Feel free to substitute other veggies that are in season to create your own version of this family-friendly recipe.

TASTY TOFU-VEGGIE *Kebabs*

MAKES 6 SERVINGS

KEBABS

12 to 14 twelve-inch bamboo skewers, soaked in water for 15 to 20 minutes, to prevent them from burning while cooking

1 block (14 to 16 ounces) extra-firm regular tofu (see note), drained, pressed (see note, page 220) and cut into cubes

10 to 12 mini sweet peppers, seeded and cut in half or 2 red and/or orange sweet bell peppers, seeded and cut into large chunks

8 ounces white button mushrooms, sliced in half (if large)

8 ounces cremini mushrooms, sliced in half (if large)

1 small yellow summer squash, sliced

1 small zucchini, sliced

14 to 16 cherry or grape tomatoes

6 to 8 Campari or small plum tomatoes, sliced in half or quartered

2 small sweet onions, cut into chunks

SAUCE

2 tablespoons extra-virgin olive oil

1 teaspoon smoked paprika

18 to 20 ounces of your favorite prepared vegan BBQ sauce or *Easiest BBQ Sauce* (page 90)

Preheat the oven to 375 degrees F. Line a very large, rimmed baking sheet (about 20- x 14-inches) with unbleached parchment paper. Evenly divide and thread the veggies and tofu onto the prepared skewers. Arrange the kebabs in a single layer on the lined baking sheet.

Brush each kebab liberally with olive oil and sprinkle with the smoked paprika. Tent with foil and bake for 30 minutes. Put the pan on a wire rack, remove the foil, and spoon or brush about one-third of the BBQ sauce over the top of the kebabs and bake for 10 minutes.

Remove the kebabs from the oven and spoon the remaining barbecue sauce over the kebabs. Increase the heat to 400 degrees F. Bake for 20 to 25 minutes or until the kebabs are golden brown. Transfer the pan to a wire rack and let cool for 5 minutes. Serve 2 skewers per person over *Basmati Rice with Cashews and Scallions* (page 249).

CHEF'S NOTE: *If you are cooking gluten free, make certain to purchase certified gluten-free tofu, available in most supermarkets.*

GLUTEN-FREE OPTION

These cheese-less burritos get their zing from shredded zucchini and spicy salsa. Topped with a vegan almond cream, these burritos are super satisfying to serve any day of the week.

BLACK BEAN-ZUCCHINI Burritos with Almond Crème Fraîche

MAKES 2 TO 4 SERVINGS

BURRITOS

1 can (15 to 16 ounces) **black beans, drained and rinsed**

5 heaping tablespoons prepared salsa, plus more as needed

1⅔ cups shredded zucchini (1 medium or 2 small), **divided**

1½ teaspoons chili powder

2 teaspoons extra-virgin olive oil

4 vegan whole-grain or gluten-free tortillas (each about 8-inches in diameter, see note)

Sliced mini sweet peppers, for garnish (optional)

ALMOND CREME FRAICHE

½ cup raw almonds

6 to 10 tablespoons water, plus more as needed

2 tablespoons freshly squeezed lemon juice

Preheat the oven to 350 degrees F. Line a 9- x 12-inch or similarly sized baking dish with aluminum foil, allowing a 5-inch overhang on the two lengthwise sides of the dish. Line the foil with unbleached parchment paper, allowing a 5-inch overhang on the two lengthwise sides of the dish. Put the black beans and salsa into a medium-sized bowl and lightly mash, using a potato masher or large fork until well combined but still chunky. Put 1⅓ cups of the shredded zucchini, chili powder and olive oil into a separate medium-sized bowl and gently stir to coat.

To assemble the first burrito, put 1 tortilla on a dinner plate. Put one-quarter of the black bean mixture in the center of the tortilla. Top with a heaping ¼ cup of the shredded zucchini/chili powder mixture. Roll the tortilla up around the filling, folding in the sides, as you go, to make a burrito. Put the burrito seam-side down in the lined pan. Repeat the process until you have formed a total of 4 burritos. Bring the sides of the parchment paper and the foil over the burritos and crimp to seal. (This will keep the burritos from drying out as they bake.) Bake for 40 to 50 minutes or until heated through. Remove from oven and carefully uncover the burritos (the steam will be very hot!). Bake for 5 minutes more, or until the tops of the tortillas are slightly golden. Put the pan on a wire rack and let cool 5 minutes before serving.

Meanwhile, to make the *Almond Crème Fraîche,* put the almonds, 6 tablespoons water and lemon juice into a blender and process until smooth and creamy, adding more water, as needed, to achieve the desired consistency.

Put 1 or 2 burritos on each plate and garnish with one-quarter of the remaining shredded zucchini and sliced mini peppers, if desired. Drizzle a generous amount of the *Almond Crème Fraîche* over the top. Serve with *Laura's Cauliflower "Rice"* (page 250) on the side and *No-Bake Cinnamon-Chocolate Pudding Cakes* (page 278) for dessert, if desired.

CHEF'S NOTE: *If preferred, you may use 10-inch tortillas to make 2 to 3 burritos instead of 4.*

"Vegetable" is the word that "vegan" is based on, and in a plant-based diet, vegetables are often featured in entrées. However, they can complement a main dish just as they do in omnivorous diets, so this chapter includes some of my favorite recipes for family-friendly vegetable side dishes. In my mind, the key to creating tasty veggie dishes is to purchase produce that's in season and/or locally grown (when available). This helps ensure that the vegetables are as fresh, flavorful and nutritious as possible. Vegetables are so colorful, too, so serving them on the side is the best way to jazz up any meal!

CHAPTER
FOURTEEN

Veggies on Parade

Salt and Pepper Steak Fries, *page 246*

GLUTEN-FREE

This is an easy side dish that makes good use of summer squash and fresh bell peppers.

ZUCCHINI, SUMMER SQUASH AND SWEET PEPPER *Sauté*

MAKES 4 SERVINGS

1 medium sweet onion, sliced

2 tablespoons extra-virgin olive oil

⅛ teaspoon crushed red pepper

1 tablespoon gluten-free tamari

¼ teaspoon garlic powder or 1 large clove garlic, minced

2 small zucchini, sliced

2 small summer squash, sliced

1 large orange or red sweet bell pepper, seeded and cut into strips

JAZZY TIP: *To decrease the fat content in many savory dishes, you can replace some or all of the oil used in stovetop cooking with vegetable broth or water. Use 3 tablespoons of either veggie broth or water to replace 1 tablespoon of oil. Unlike oil, these liquids will evaporate during cooking, so be very watchful and add more as needed.*

Put the onion, olive oil and crushed red pepper into a sauté pan. Cover and cook over medium heat, stirring occasionally, for about 7 minutes or until the onion becomes slightly translucent. Add the tamari, garlic, zucchini, summer squash and sweet pepper. Cover and cook, stirring occasionally, for about 6 minutes or until the squash and pepper are both cooked *al dente*. Serve immediately.

GLUTEN-FREE

Beautiful colors and inviting flavors will make this hearty side dish a keeper in your recipe box.

Confetti BROCCOLI RABE

MAKES 4 SERVINGS

- 1 large bunch broccoli rabe, trimmed and chopped
- 1 can (15 to 16 ounces) chickpeas (garbanzo beans) drained and rinsed
- ¾ cup seeded and diced red sweet bell pepper
- ½ cup vegetable broth, plus more as needed
- 1 tablespoon extra-virgin olive oil
- 2 small cloves garlic, minced
- 1½ tablespoons nonpareil capers, drained and rinsed
- ¼ teaspoon crushed red pepper
- ½ teaspoon gluten-free tamari

Put the broccoli rabe, chickpeas, red pepper, vegetable broth, olive oil, garlic, capers and crushed red pepper into a large skillet. Cover and cook over medium-low heat for 10 minutes, stirring often and adding more broth as needed to prevent sticking. Add the tamari and cook, stirring frequently, for 3 to 5 minutes, or until the broccoli rabe is crisp tender but still bright green. Serve immediately.

GLUTEN-FREE

This fragrant roasted asparagus makes a delicious side dish. Garam masala is a mixture of ground spices used in Indian cuisine. This enticing spice blend has a slightly sweet flavor enhanced by a touch of black pepper with subtle notes of cumin, coriander and turmeric.

Garam Masala ASPARAGUS

MAKES 4 SERVINGS

- **1 medium bunch asparagus, washed with tough ends removed** (see note)
- **½ tablespoon extra-virgin olive oil**
- **½ to 1 teaspoon garam masala, to taste**
- **¼ teaspoon sea salt, plus more as needed**

Preheat the oven to 400 degrees F. Line a large, rimmed baking pan with unbleached parchment paper. Put the asparagus in a large bowl. Drizzle the olive oil over the top of the asparagus and gently toss to lightly coat the asparagus stalks with the oil. Add the garam masala and salt and toss to coat. Arrange the asparagus in an even layer on the lined pan. Bake for 6 to 12 minutes (depending on the thickness of the asparagus), until asparagus is crisp tender. Sprinkle with more salt, to taste, while still hot. Serve warm.

CHEF'S NOTE: *The end of each asparagus stalk is very tough, so it must be removed before cooking. To do so, pick up each asparagus stalk and gently bend the bottom of the asparagus stalk until the tough end easily snaps off.*

3 INGREDIENTS OR LESS

GLUTEN-FREE

Just three ingredients make this holiday staple an easy side dish to serve any time of year. The maple syrup helps to caramelize the Brussels sprouts as they roast, while the chili powder adds a touch of subtle heat. Bonus: this dish is ready for the oven in less than ten minutes.

Chili-Maple BRUSSELS SPROUTS

MAKES 4 SERVINGS

24 ounces Brussels sprouts, washed, trimmed and cut in half

2 tablespoons maple syrup

2 teaspoons chili powder

Preheat the oven to 375 degrees F. Line a large, rimmed baking pan with unbleached parchment paper. Put all of the ingredients in a medium-sized bowl. Toss gently until the Brussels sprouts are evenly coated. Spread the Brussels sprouts in an even layer on the prepared pan. Roast for 30 to 35 minutes or until they are soft and golden brown around the edges, turning once while cooking. Serve warm.

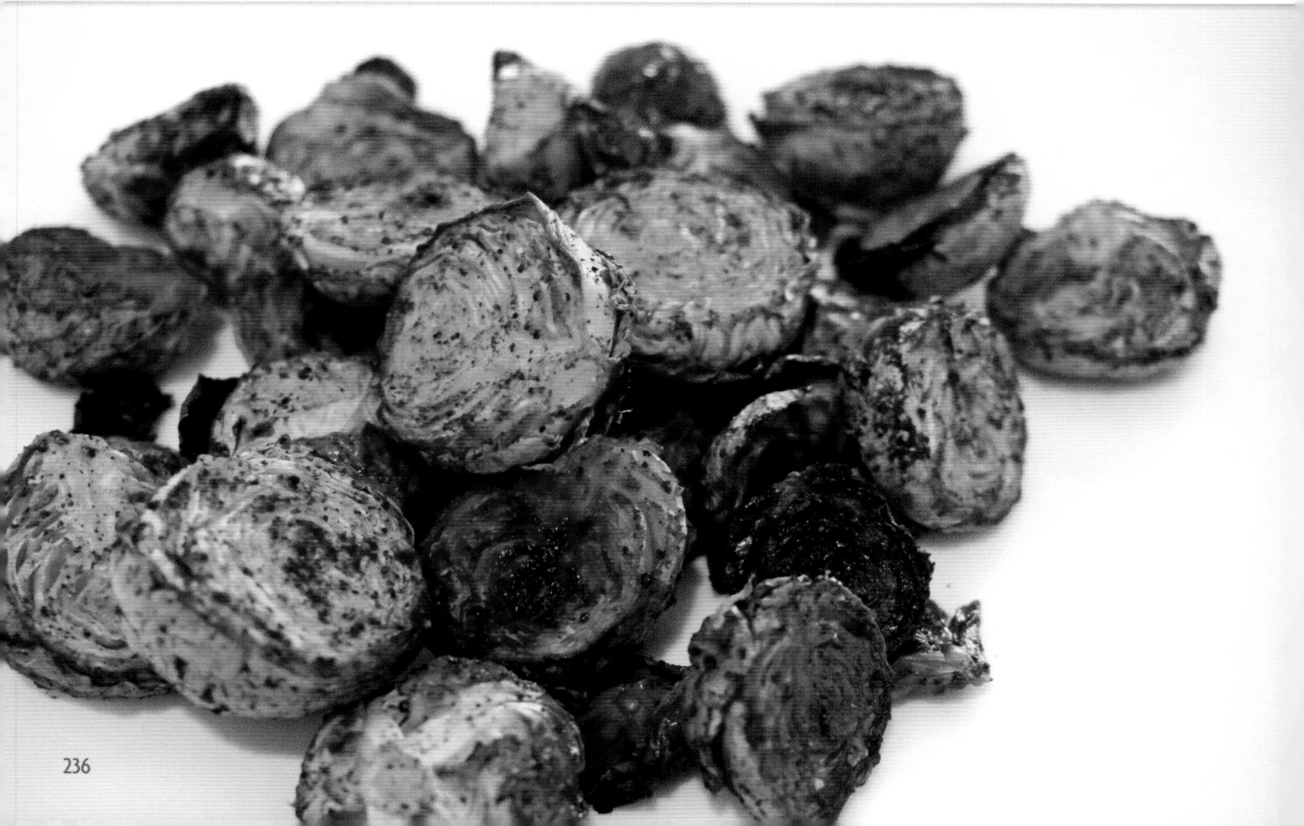

GLUTEN-FREE

These cute little artichokes come together for the oven in one, two, three! Tossed with a few basic ingredients, these mini beauties roast up harmoniously to make a lovely side dish.

ROASTED BABY *Artichokes*

MAKES 4 SERVINGS

- 8 or 9 baby artichokes, washed well
- 2 tablespoons balsamic vinegar
- 1 tablespoon extra-virgin olive oil
- 2 teaspoons Italian seasoning blend
- ¼ teaspoon garlic powder
- ¼ teaspoon sea salt

Preheat the oven to 400 degrees F. Line a large, rimmed baking sheet with unbleached parchment paper. Slice off the sharp tops of the baby artichokes. Slice the artichokes in half lengthwise. Put the artichokes and remaining ingredients in a large bowl and toss to combine. Arrange the artichokes flat side down on the prepared baking sheet.

Bake for 30 minutes, tenting with foil for the last 10 to 15 minutes of cooking. Serve warm, or store in a tightly covered container and refrigerate for 2 to 4 hours and serve cold.

GLUTEN-FREE

This appealing side dish will enhance any meal. It also makes a great introduction to cooking kale, as it takes the mystery out of preparing this fantastically nutritious leafy green vegetable.

Sweet and Savory KALE

MAKES 4 TO 6 SERVINGS

1 very large bunch kale, de-stemmed, thoroughly washed and *very* thinly sliced (see note)

1½ tablespoons extra-virgin olive oil

2 teaspoons brown sugar or 1 tablespoon maple syrup

2 teaspoons gluten-free tamari, plus more to taste

4 teaspoons roasted or raw sunflower seeds (salted or unsalted)

Fit a steamer basket into a large saucepan with a tight-fitting lid. Add 2 to 3 inches of cold water, and then add the kale. Cover and bring to a boil. Steam the kale until wilted and quite soft but still bright green, 6 to 8 minutes. Transfer to a medium-sized bowl. Put the olive oil, brown sugar (or maple syrup) and tamari in a small bowl and briskly whisk to combine. Pour the olive oil mixture over the kale and toss until the kale is evenly coated. Sprinkle the sunflower seeds over the kale and toss lightly. Taste and add more tamari, if desired. Serve immediately.

CHEF'S NOTE: *Thoroughly cleaning dark leafy greens—such as kale, spinach, dandelion greens and collard greens—is essential, as they often have sandy residue buried in the leaves. To clean leafy greens, start by putting the greens in a very large bowl and cover them with cold water. Swish the greens around gently, scoop them out of the bowl and put them in a large colander (in the sink) to drain. Empty the bowl and rinse it well. Repeat these steps until there is no sand or dirt in the bottom of the bowl after you remove the greens. If you are using the greens raw (such as in a salad) dry them thoroughly, using a salad spinner or paper towels. If you are cooking the greens, there's no need to dry them. The droplets of water that remain on the leaves (after rinsing) will help the greens stay moist while cooking.*

See photo of this recipe on page 208.

GLUTEN-FREE

This satisfying side dish is an excellent way to sneak spinach into your family's meals!

SNEAKY SPINACH *Mash-up*

MAKES 4 SERVINGS

- 4 medium white or yellow potatoes, peeled and chopped
- 1 medium turnip, peeled and chopped
- ½ to 1 cup water
- ½ large (or 1 small) vegan gluten-free bouillon cube, crumbled
- 4 ounces baby spinach
- 1 tablespoon vegan buttery spread
- Sea salt, to taste
- Freshly ground black pepper, to taste

Put the potatoes and turnips into a medium-sized saucepan and add about ½ cup water to reach 2-inches in depth. Cover and bring to a boil over medium-high heat. Decrease the heat to medium-low, cover and cook for 15 to 17 minutes or until the potatoes and turnips are almost soft, adding a bit more water, 3 tablespoons at a time, if the pan starts to become dry.

Add the spinach, cover and cook for 1 minute. Remove the pan from the heat and add the vegan buttery spread. Using a potato masher, mash the veggies together, making certain to incorporate the spinach into the potatoes and turnips. Season with salt and pepper to taste and serve.

Sneaky Spinach Mash-Up served with *BBQ Cauliflower Cutlets* (page 212).

GLUTEN-FREE

These little darlings are a fun and flavorful way to present potatoes. The inside pulp stays nice and tender while the outside gets crispy. Serve these on the side for any party meal, even breakfast!

ROSEMARY *Smashed* POTATOES

MAKES 6 TO 8 SERVINGS

35 to 40 ounces fingerling or baby potatoes, scrubbed

1½ tablespoons extra-virgin olive oil

1 tablespoon crushed dried rosemary

½ teaspoon sea salt, plus more as needed

Fit a steamer basket into a medium-sized saucepan with a tight-fitting lid. Add 2 to 3 inches of cold water to the pot and then add the potatoes. Cover and bring to a boil. Steam the potatoes for 10 minutes or until they are *almost* fork tender. Transfer the potatoes to a large bowl and let cool 10 minutes.

While the potatoes cool, preheat the oven to 375 degrees F. Line a large, rimmed baking sheet with unbleached parchment paper. Add the olive oil, rosemary and sea salt to the cooled potatoes and toss to lightly coat, using a large spoon, letting the excess olive oil and rosemary run to the bottom of the bowl. Arrange the potatoes about ½-inch apart in a single layer on the prepared baking sheet. Using a sturdy, flat spatula, "smash" each potato so it is slightly flattened. Brush the tops of the flattened potatoes with the seasoned oil that settled into the bottom of the mixing bowl.

Roast for 50 to 60 minutes or until the potatoes are golden brown and slightly crispy. Season with more sea salt, if desired, while still hot. Let cool 5 to 10 minutes and serve warm.

GLUTEN-FREE

These tender and flavorful baby spuds are baked in the oven with a zingy mustard sauce, making a festive side dish for any supper.

Tiny Potatoes WITH SPICY MUSTARD SAUCE

MAKES 4 TO 6 SERVINGS

SAUCE

3 tablespoons spicy brown mustard

2 tablespoons extra-virgin olive oil

1 tablespoon maple syrup

1 teaspoon Italian seasoning blend

¼ teaspoon garlic powder

¼ teaspoon sea salt

Dash cayenne

POTATOES

2 pounds baby red and/or yellow potatoes, scrubbed with larger potatoes cut in half

Preheat the oven to 375 degrees F. Line a large, rimmed baking pan with unbleached parchment paper.

Put the sauce ingredients into a small bowl and stir until combined. Put the potatoes into a large bowl, add the sauce and stir to combine. Arrange the potatoes in a single layer on the prepared baking pan. Bake for 35 to 45 minutes or until the potatoes are very tender. Put the pan on a wire rack and let cool 5 to 10 minutes. Serve warm.

GLUTEN-FREE

Maple syrup helps bring out the natural flavor of the sweet potato in this easy, three-ingredient side dish.

Mashed MAPLE SWEET POTATOES

MAKES 4 SERVINGS

- 4 medium/large sweet potatoes, peeled and cubed
- 1 tablespoon maple syrup, plus more as needed
- Sea salt, to taste

Fit a steamer basket into a medium-sized saucepan with a tight-fitting lid. Add 2 to 3 inches of cold water, and then add the sweet potatoes. Cover and bring to a boil. Steam for 15 to 20 minutes or until fork tender. Transfer the sweet potatoes to a medium-sized bowl and add the maple syrup. Mash until almost smooth, using a potato masher. Taste and add more maple syrup, if desired. Season with salt to taste and serve.

GLUTEN-FREE

I love replacing traditional fries with this squash version, and my husband likes 'em, too. It's a great way to get the kiddos to eat squash! If you *are* making this for kids, leave out the chili powder and garlic (or use less of each) and your family will welcome this spin on a common side dish.

SUMMER SQUASH "French" Fries

MAKES 2 TO 4 SERVINGS

- 2 medium zucchini, cut into thick matchsticks
- 2 medium summer squash, cut into thick matchsticks
- 1 tablespoon extra-virgin olive oil, plus more as needed
- 1 teaspoon chili powder
- ½ teaspoon garlic powder
- ½ teaspoon sea salt
- Freshly ground black pepper, to taste

Preheat the oven to 425 degrees F. Line a large, rimmed baking pan with unbleached parchment paper. Put the squash "fries" into a large bowl. Sprinkle with 1 tablespoon olive oil, chili powder, garlic powder, sea salt and pepper and stir to combine. (If the squash fries still seem a bit dry, add 1 more tablespoon olive oil.) Arrange the fries in a single layer on the prepared pan. Bake for 15 to 25 minutes or until the fries are brown around the edges. Serve immediately.

JAZZY TIP: *Buying fresh produce from your local farmers' market is a wonderful way to support small farmers and keep the money you are spending in your community.*

GLUTEN-FREE

These tantalizing fries are baked instead of fried, but they taste like the classic version you'd find in a New York steakhouse. Seasoned with a generous amount of salt and pepper, these fries make an excellent companion to a morning scramble, veggie burger or a main dish salad.

SALT AND PEPPER *Steak Fries*

MAKES 4 TO 6 SERVINGS

- 6 large red potatoes
- 2 tablespoons extra-virgin olive oil
- Several generous grinds coarse sea salt, to taste
- Several generous grinds black pepper, to taste

Preheat the oven to 425 degrees F. Line a large, rimmed baking sheet with unbleached parchment paper. Cut the potatoes into wedges, much like the shape of a traditional steak fry. Put the potato wedges into a large bowl. Add the olive oil and stir to coat. Add liberal amounts of salt and pepper to taste. Arrange the fries in a single layer on the prepared baking pan. Bake for 30 to 50 minutes or until the fries are golden and crispy around the edges. Put the pan on a wire rack and add more salt, if desired. Let cool for 5 minutes. Serve warm.

Salt and Pepper Steak Fries served with *"Hungry Guy" Burgers* (page 159).

Photo courtesy of Annie Olivero. Learn more about Annie on page 296.

This flavorful rice makes a wonderful accompaniment to any meal.

Basmati Rice WITH CASHEWS AND SCALLIONS

MAKES 4 SERVINGS

2¼ cups water (see note)

1 cup *uncooked* brown basmati rice, rinsed and drained

½ large vegan gluten-free bouillon cube (or 1 small cube)

⅓ cup chopped roasted and salted cashews, plus more for serving

1 large or 2 small scallion(s)**, thinly sliced, divided**

Put the water, rice and bouillon into a medium-sized saucepan. Cover and bring to a boil over medium-high heat. Decrease the heat to medium-low, cover and cook for 35 to 40 minutes or until all of the liquid is absorbed. Fluff the rice with a fork and remove from the heat. Fold in the cashews and two-thirds of the sliced scallions. Cover and let stand 5 to 10 minutes. Serve garnished with more chopped cashews and the remaining sliced scallions.

CHEF'S NOTE: *If you prefer firmer rice, decrease the water to 2 cups.*

GLUTEN-FREE

When I see organic cauliflower on sale or find it freshly picked at the farmers market, I like to make this dish. Simply shred the cauliflower and briefly cook it, making a satisfying substitute for brown or white rice.

Laura's CAULIFLOWER "RICE"

MAKES 4 SERVINGS

- 1 medium cauliflower, tough core removed and leaves trimmed (see note)
- 2 to 4 teaspoons extra-virgin olive oil, plus more as needed
- 2 tablespoons water (or vegetable broth), plus more as needed
- ½ teaspoon gluten-free tamari, plus more as needed
- Freshly ground black pepper, to taste
- ⅛ teaspoon sea salt, plus more to taste
- 1 tablespoon freshly chopped parsley (optional)
- ½ tablespoon vegan buttery spread

Grate the cauliflower into little pieces of "rice" using the medium-sized holes of a box grater, or cut into florets and pulse in a food processor (see note). Put the cauliflower "rice," olive oil and 2 tablespoons water (or vegetable broth) in a large sauté pan. Cover and cook for 2 to 3 minutes over medium heat, stirring occasionally. Add more water, olive oil or broth if the pan becomes dry.

Add the tamari, black pepper and sea salt and cook for 3 to 4 minutes or until the cauliflower starts to soften, adding more water and/or oil if the pan becomes dry. Stir in the optional chopped parsley and cook for an additional 2 to 4 minutes, stirring often, and adding more water if the pan becomes dry. Turn off the heat and stir in the vegan buttery spread to evenly coat the "rice." Serve warm.

CHEF'S NOTE: *If you use a food processor to make your cauliflower rice, make certain to not over-process, or you will have cauliflower mush!*

CHEF'S NOTE: *You may use a white or orange cauliflower in this recipe. Photo on opposite page uses an orange cauliflower.*

Serving a dreamy, sweet vegan dessert need not be challenging. In this chapter I have included some of my favorite rich-tasting confections, all designed to surprise and satisfy your family and friends. These delectable desserts are dairy-free, egg-free and 100% vegan! From luscious cakes to scrumptious cookies to mini pies and fruit desserts, be sure to give these outstanding treats a try!

CHAPTER
FIFTEEN
Sweet Dreams ARE MADE OF THIS

Lemon-Raspberry Swirl Cheeze-Cake, *page 254*

GLUTEN-FREE OPTION

This amazing dairy free, vegan cheesecake tastes incredibly creamy and delicious. It's a fruity, sweet dessert that makes a gorgeous presentation to impress your family and guests!

LEMON-RASPBERRY SWIRL Cheeze-Cake

MAKES 8 TO 10 SERVINGS

FILLING

1 cup chopped or halved raw cashews

½ cup water

1 block (14 to 16 ounces) extra-firm regular tofu (see note)

½ cup freshly squeezed lemon juice (about 3 medium lemons)

2 tablespoons gluten-free, quick cooking rolled oats

1 cup vegan cane sugar or raw cane turbinado sugar

1/16 rounded teaspoon ground turmeric

CRUST

2 rounded tablespoons vegan buttery spread, plus more to coat pan

1½ cups vegan lemon or ginger cookie crumbs (about 20 to 25 cookies, see note)

RASPBERRY SWIRL

3 rounded tablespoons seedless raspberry jam

Scant ½ tablespoon water

Put the cashews and ½ cup water into a small bowl. Refrigerate for 2 to 4 hours.

Preheat the oven to 375 degrees F. Generously coat the bottom and sides of a 9-inch round springform pan with vegan buttery spread. To make the crust, put the cookie crumbs in a medium-sized bowl and add 2 rounded tablespoons vegan buttery spread. Combine using a dough blender until the mixture resembles wet sand. Evenly press the mixture into the prepared pan, using the bottom of a measuring cup to flatten the crust into an even layer. Pre-bake the crust for 5 to 6 minutes. Put the pan on a wire rack and let cool for 10 minutes while you make the filling.

To make the filling, drain the cashews (that have been soaking) and rinse thoroughly in cold water. Put the drained and soaked cashews, tofu, lemon juice, oats, sugar and turmeric in a blender container. Process for 30 seconds to 1 minute, or until completely smooth. Pour the mixture over the cooled crust and smooth out the top using a rubber spatula.

To make the raspberry swirl, put the raspberry jam and water into a small bowl and vigorously stir to combine. Carefully spoon long, thin lines of the raspberry jam mixture over the top of the cheeze-cake, about 5 to 6 "lines" in all. Then, using a wooden skewer or the tip of a knife, gently *swirl* the raspberry jam into the top of the cheesecake in a pleasing, marbleized pattern. Put the cheeze-cake on a rectangular sheet pan (to catch any drips) and bake for 35 to 45 minutes or until the center is

almost firm to the touch. (The raspberry filling will be *very* soft at this point, but it will firm up once the cheeze-cake chills in the refrigerator).

Put the cheeze-cake on a wire rack. Immediately and gently run a table knife around the perimeter of the cheeze-cake. Let the cheeze-cake cool for 30 minutes, and then *carefully* remove the springform rim. Serve warm (the cheeze-cake will still be *very* soft) or to serve cold, loosely cover and refrigerate for 4 to 6 hours or overnight. (The cheeze-cake will firm up when chilled.)

CHEF'S NOTE: *If you are cooking gluten free, make certain to purchase certified gluten-free tofu and vegan, gluten-free cookies, available in many supermarkets.*

Wow! This cake looks absolutely beautiful. With a hint of coconut, this moist and delicious cake makes an impressive dessert for family and guests alike.

Delectable PINEAPPLE UPSIDE-DOWN CAKE

MAKES 8 SERVINGS

- 2 tablespoons plus 2 teaspoons vegan buttery spread, melted
- 4 tablespoons vegan dark brown sugar
- 7 to 8 slices canned, unsweetened pineapple, well-drained, with juice and remaining slices reserved
- 5 Medjool dates, each chopped into thirds
- 1½ cups unbleached all-purpose flour or whole wheat flour
- 1 cup vegan cane sugar
- ½ cup unsweetened shredded dried coconut
- 1 teaspoon baking soda
- 1 teaspoon baking powder
- ⅛ teaspoon sea salt
- ½ cup plus 2 tablespoons reserved pineapple juice
- ½ cup unsweetened nondairy milk
- ¼ cup extra-virgin olive oil
- ½ cup diced canned pineapple (from the reserved slices)

CHEF'S NOTE: *This cake becomes very crisp and dark brown on the outside as it bakes, but if it starts to* burn *in the last 20 minutes of baking, loosely tent it with some foil.*

Preheat the oven to 350 degrees F. Pour the melted buttery spread into a 9-inch round cake pan. Using a pastry brush, spread the buttery spread evenly over the bottom and up the sides of the pan, to coat. Evenly distribute the brown sugar over the melted buttery spread. Arrange 7 to 8 pineapple slices in an even layer over the brown sugar. Put one piece of chopped date into the center of each pineapple, and then arrange the other date pieces in the "empty" spaces that surround the pineapple slices.

Put the flour, sugar, coconut, baking soda, baking powder and salt into a large bowl and mix together using a dry whisk until well combined. Make a well in the center of the bowl. Add the pineapple juice, nondairy milk and olive oil and stir with a large spoon to make a batter. Fold in the diced pineapple. Pour the batter into the prepared pan.

Bake for 5 minutes, and then decrease the heat to 325 degrees F and bake for 55 to 70 minutes, or until a toothpick inserted into the center of the cake comes out clean, the top of the cake feels *very firm* to the touch and the cake is dark golden brown (see note). Put the cake on a wire rack and let cool for 45 minutes to 1 hour. Once the cake is cool enough to handle, *carefully* invert it onto a serving platter. Let cool completely, slice and serve. Store leftover cake tightly covered in the refrigerator for up to 3 days.

This rich, dense and decadent two-layer beauty, piled high with luscious frosting and topped with juicy strawberries, was first created for my sister's birthday party last year. Yes, it has many (many) steps and a *zillion* calories, but it's well worth the effort for a festive event!

Berrylicious OLIVE OIL CAKE

MAKES 14 TO 16 SERVINGS

FROSTING

4½ cups vegan confectioner's (powdered) sugar

⅔ cup vegan buttery spread

1½ teaspoons vanilla extract

2 to 4 tablespoons sweetened vanilla-flavored nondairy milk

CAKE

½ cup extra-virgin olive oil, plus more to coat pans (see note)

2½ cups whole wheat flour, plus more to coat pans

1⅓ cups raw cane turbinado sugar or vegan cane sugar

1 teaspoon baking powder

1 teaspoon baking soda

½ teaspoon sea salt

2 cups unsweetened nondairy milk

1¼ tablespoons freshly squeezed lemon juice

2 teaspoons vanilla extract

FILLING AND TOPPING

3 to 4 heaping tablespoons seedless strawberry preserves or jam

12 to 16 (1 to 1½ pints) large strawberries, de-stemmed and cut in half

To make the frosting, put the powdered sugar and vegan buttery spread in a medium-sized bowl and mix with a spoon until there are no lumps (see note). Stir in the vanilla and 1 tablespoon of the nondairy milk. Gradually beat in just enough nondairy milk to make the frosting smooth and spreadable. (If the frosting becomes too thin, beat in a bit more powdered sugar.) Cover and refrigerate the frosting for 2 to 3 hours, or until it firms up enough to pipe onto the cake.

CHEF'S NOTE: *If preferred you can mix the frosting in an electric mixer on low speed.*

To make the cake, preheat the oven to 350 degrees F. Generously oil two 9-inch round cake pans and line the bottoms with a round of unbleached parchment paper. Brush a bit more olive oil over the parchment, and then lightly coat the paper and inside rims of each pan with flour (see note on page 260). Put the flour, sugar, baking powder, baking soda and salt into a large bowl and stir with a dry whisk to combine. Make a well in the center of the bowl. Add the nondairy milk, ½ cup olive oil, lemon juice and vanilla and stir with a large spoon to thoroughly combine.

CHEF'S NOTE: *If preferred you can use vegan buttery spread to oil the cake pans.*

(Recipe continues on page 260.)

CHEF'S NOTE: *To "dust" a cake pan, add a tablespoon of flour to the oiled pan (and parchment) and gently shake it around the pan until the interior surface is lightly covered. Angle the pan over a bowl or the sink and gently tap out any excess flour.*

Pour one-half of the batter into each of the prepared cake pans and tap lightly on the counter to remove air bubbles. Bake 25 to 35 minutes or until a toothpick inserted in the center of each cake comes out clean. Put the pans on a wire rack and gently loosen the sides of the cakes with a knife. Cool for 5 to 7 minutes and carefully invert each cake round onto the rack. Peel off the parchment and carefully invert each cake again, so the top is facing upward. Let cool completely (about 2 hours) before frosting the cakes.

To keep your serving plate from getting covered with frosting, place unbleached parchment paper strips around the edge of a pretty plate. Place one of the cake rounds on the prepared plate. (Level the cake slightly with a serrated knife, if needed to make a flat surface.) Spoon half of the preserves (or jam) over the cake in a thin, even layer using an offset spatula. Pipe an even circular layer of the frosting over the preserves and put the second cake layer on the frosting, gently pressing down, so the layer will adhere. Spoon the remaining half of the preserves over the second cake layer and spread in an even layer.

Using a medium-large star piping tip, pipe a border of "stars" around the outer perimeter of the cake by holding your piping bag at a direct 90-degree angle and gently squeezing out a "star" shape. Release pressure and pull your piping bag away from the cake. Continue in this manner to pipe "stars" around the entire outer border of the cake. Then pipe an *inner* circle of "stars" on top of the cake (see photo). Snuggle fresh strawberries in between the "star" frosting circles. Pipe more "stars" around the bottom of your cake, alternating them with strawberries halves or slices.

Refrigerate for at least 2 hours to allow frosting to firm up. Remove the cake from the refrigerator about 5 to 7 minutes before serving. Cut into slices, and finally, it's ready to serve! Covered tightly and stored in the refrigerator, leftover cake will keep for 1 to 2 days.

GLUTEN-FREE

Oh yes! So healthy, but so tasty too, these colorful, semi-sweet jewels whip up in a flash for a quick snack or after supper treat. Bonus: They make a wonderful holiday cookie, too!

BANANA-CRANBERRY Oat Cookies

MAKES 12 COOKIES

- **1 large, ripe banana, peeled**
- **2 tablespoons maple syrup** (see note)
- **½ teaspoon ground cinnamon**
- **1 cup gluten-free, old fashioned rolled oats**
- **⅓ cup sweetened dried cranberries** (see note)
- **¼ cup unsweetened shredded dried coconut**

Preheat the oven to 400 degrees F. Line a large, rimmed baking pan with unbleached parchment paper. Put the banana, maple syrup and ground cinnamon in a medium-sized bowl and mash until almost smooth, using a potato masher. Add the oats, cranberries and coconut and stir to combine.

For each cookie, put 1 heaping tablespoon of the dough on the lined baking sheet and flatten slightly. Bake for 10 to 12 minutes or until golden around the edges. Put the pan on a wire rack and let cool for 5 minutes. Transfer the cookies to the wire rack and let cool 10 minutes before serving. Stored tightly covered in the refrigerator, cookies will keep for 3 or 4 days.

CHEF'S NOTE: *These cookies are not overly sweet. If you prefer a sweeter cookie, stir in 2 tablespoons vegan cane sugar or brown sugar to the banana mixture before you add the oats.*

CHEF'S NOTE: *You may use raisins in place of the cranberries, if desired.*

See photo of this recipe on page 262.

Banana-Cranberry Oat Cookies *(page 261), above*

Peanut Butter and Jelly Cookies *(page 263), below*

GLUTEN-FREE OPTION

Like peanut butter and jelly sandwiches packed into sweet cookie confections, these gems truly shine. With a delectable jelly center and crisp base, they make the perfect afternoon snack paired with a tall glass of nondairy milk.

Peanut Butter and Jelly COOKIES

MAKES 18 COOKIES

- **1 cup whole wheat flour** (see note for gluten-free option)
- **½ teaspoon baking powder**
- **⅛ teaspoon sea salt**
- **⅛ cup creamy peanut butter**
- **⅓ cup maple syrup**
- **3 tablespoons sweetened plain or vanilla-flavored nondairy milk**
- **1 teaspoon vanilla extract**
- **½ to ⅔ cup raspberry, strawberry or blueberry preserves, jelly or jam**

Preheat the oven to 375 degrees F. Line a large baking sheet with unbleached parchment paper.

Put the flour, baking powder and salt in a medium-sized bowl and stir with a dry whisk to combine. Add the peanut butter, maple syrup, nondairy milk and vanilla extract to the flour mixture and stir vigorously until thoroughly combined. The dough will be stiff.

For each cookie, drop about 1 tablespoon of the dough onto the prepared baking sheet, using a cookie scoop or rounded spoon. With your thumb, press down gently into the middle of each cookie, making a small well. Fill each well with about 1 teaspoon of the preserves.

Bake for 14 to 18 minutes or until the cookies are golden brown around the edges. Put the baking sheet on a wire rack. Let the cookies cool on the baking sheet for 10 to 15 minutes before transferring directly to the rack to cool further. Stored in an airtight container in the refrigerator, the cookies will keep for about 3 days.

CHEF'S NOTE: *For a gluten-free option, use a "1-to-1" variety of gluten-free flour in place of the whole wheat flour, adding an additional 2 tablespoons of the gluten-free flour,* if needed to make it a cookie-dough consistency. *Once the dough is thoroughly mixed, refrigerate for 50 minutes to 1 hour. Bake as directed. To give the cookies extra crunch, sprinkle each cookie with a bit of vegan cane sugar before adding the preserves. (Thank you to Chef Carol Smolinski for contributing the gluten-free option and tips for this recipe!)*

This recipe is revised from *Laura Theodore's Jazzy Vegetarian Classics: Vegan Twists on American Family Favorites (BenBella Books, 2013).* Reprinted with permission. Learn more at www.benbellabooks.com.

GLUTEN-FREE OPTION

These *jazzylicious* vegan oatmeal cookies feature a crisp outside and super moist center. Ripe, mashed bananas stand in for the eggs and sweet raisins add punch. This cookie is a real classic!

OATMEAL-RAISIN Cookies

MAKES 34 TO 38 COOKIES

- 1½ cups gluten-free, quick cooking rolled oats
- ¾ cup whole wheat flour (see note for gluten-free option)
- ½ cup plus 2 tablespoons vegan cane sugar
- ¾ teaspoon ground cinnamon
- ½ teaspoon baking soda
- ½ teaspoon sea salt
- 1 cup ripe, peeled and mashed bananas
- ¼ cup plus 2 tablespoons, room temperature vegan buttery spread
- 2 to 3 tablespoons unsweetened nondairy milk
- ⅔ cup dark raisins

VARIATION: *Chocolate Chip Oatmeal Cookies: substitute vegan dark chocolate chips for the raisins.*

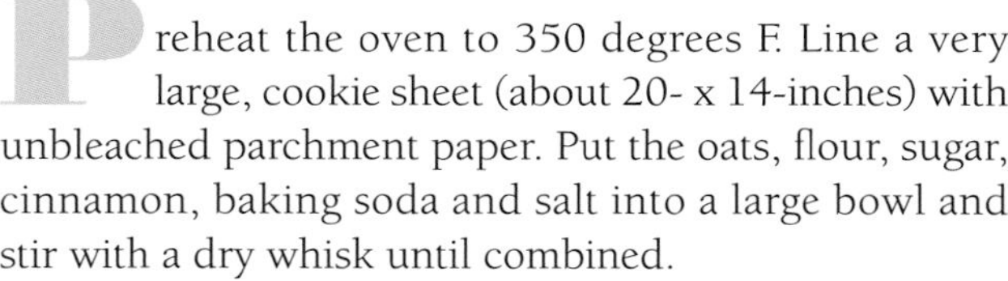

Preheat the oven to 350 degrees F. Line a very large, cookie sheet (about 20- x 14-inches) with unbleached parchment paper. Put the oats, flour, sugar, cinnamon, baking soda and salt into a large bowl and stir with a dry whisk until combined.

Put the mashed banana and buttery spread into a medium-sized bowl and mash together using a potato masher or large fork until well-combined and only small flecks of the vegan buttery spread are visible. Add the banana mixture to the dry ingredients and stir together using a large spoon until the dough starts to come together. Add 2 tablespoons of nondairy milk and stir to combine. (If the dough seems dry, add 1 more tablespoon of nondairy milk.) Fold in the raisins.

Using a 1 tablespoon cookie scoop, drop the dough onto the lined cookie sheet, spacing about ½-inch apart. Bake for 8 minutes. Put the sheet on a wire rack and gently flatten the top of each cookie slightly with a flat spatula. Bake for an additional 6 to 7 minutes or until the bottom of the cookies are golden, but the tops are still a nice blonde color. Remove from the oven and transfer the cookies to a wire rack. Cool for 15 minutes before serving. Stored in a tightly covered container, leftover cookies will keep at room temperature for up to 2 days.

CHEF'S NOTE: *For a gluten-free option, use a "1-to-1" variety of gluten-free flour in place of the whole wheat flour.*

GLUTEN-FREE

Flaxseeds stand in for egg whites in this recipe, while garbanzo bean flour helps to bind them. The result is a flawless macaroon that is egg, dairy and gluten free! Now that *is* jazzy.

COCONUT Vegaroons

MAKES 24 COOKIES

- 2 tablespoons golden flaxseeds
- ¼ cup plus 1 tablespoon water
- 1⅓ cups unsweetened shredded dried coconut
- ½ cup plus 2 tablespoons vegan cane sugar or maple sugar
- 2 tablespoons garbanzo bean (chickpea) flour
- ⅛ teaspoon sea salt
- 2 tablespoons sweetened vanilla-flavored nondairy milk
- 1¼ teaspoons vanilla extract

Preheat the oven to 325 degrees F. Line a large baking sheet with unbleached parchment paper.

Put the flaxseeds in a high-performance blender or grain mill and process into fine flour.

Transfer to a small bowl. Stir in the water and whisk vigorously to combine. Let the flaxseed mixture stand for 10 minutes while prepping the rest of the ingredients.

Put the coconut, sugar, garbanzo bean flour and salt in a large bowl and stir with a dry whisk to combine. Add the flaxseed mixture, nondairy milk and vanilla extract and stir until well blended.

For each cookie, drop 1 heaping tablespoonful of the dough onto the lined baking sheet with a cookie scoop or rounded spoon, spacing them about 1 inch apart. Flatten each macaroon slightly using a spatula. Bake for 15 minutes. Decrease the oven temperature to 300 degrees F and bake for 12 to 15 minutes or until slightly golden brown. Put the baking sheet on a wire rack. Let the cookies cool on the baking sheet for 5 minutes before transferring them to the wire rack to cool completely. Stored in an airtight container in the refrigerator, the cookies will keep for 4 days.

Sweet potatoes become a yummy dessert when combined with a bit of cinnamon and maple syrup and baked in a crisp cookie crust. These cutie pies are a wonderful way to change up your dessert at holiday time in place of pumpkin pie, and they're so easy to prepare, too!

MAPLE-SWEET POTATO Mini-Pies

MAKES 6 SERVINGS

FILLING

3 cups baked and chilled sweet potatoes (about 1½ large or 2 medium-large potatoes, see notes)

3 tablespoons maple syrup

¾ teaspoon ground cinnamon, divided (see note)

2 tablespoons whole wheat flour, gluten-free oat flour or gluten-free "1-to-1" flour

CRUST

1¼ cups vegan ginger cookie crumbs (use gluten-free cookies if you are gluten-free)

3 rounded tablespoons vegan buttery spread, plus more for coating muffin tin

TOPPING

6 pecan halves

3 tablespoons maple syrup

CHEF'S NOTE: *For a holiday dessert, use Mom's Pumpkin Pie Spice (page 97) in place of the cinnamon, if desired.*

Preheat the oven to 375 degrees F. Lightly coat a 6-cup jumbo muffin tin with vegan buttery spread. Line each cup with two 2- x 6-inch criss-crossed parchment paper strips (see photo). To make the filling, cut each cold sweet potato in half lengthwise and scoop out the pulp. Put the sweet potato pulp, 3 tablespoons maple syrup and ¼ heaping teaspoon ground cinnamon into a medium-sized bowl and mash using a potato masher or large fork until combined. Add the flour to the sweet potato mixture and stir to combine.

To make the crust, put the cookie crumbs and vegan buttery spread into a medium-sized bowl and combine using a dough blender until the mixture resembles wet sand, adding a bit more vegan buttery spread if needed. Divide the crust ingredients evenly among the 6 muffin cups and press the crust evenly into the bottom of each cup. Fill each muffin cup with one-sixth of the filling and smooth the top. Sprinkle the top of each mini pie with about 1⁄16 teaspoon of cinnamon. Bake for 35 minutes.

Put the pan on a wire rack and gently run a knife around the perimeter of each mini pie. Put the remaining 3 tablespoons maple syrup into a small bowl. Top each little pie with 1 pecan half. Using a pastry brush or small spoon, spread about ½ tablespoon of maple syrup over the top of each sweet potato pie. Let cool 30 minutes. Using the paper strips, lift each pie out of the muffin cups. Carefully peel back and remove the paper strips from each pie. (The pies will be *very* soft while warm, so you may need to re-shape them a bit at this point.)

Put the pies on a serving plate and serve warm, or loosely cover the pies and refrigerate for 4 to 6 hours to firm up and serve cold. Covered tightly and stored in the refrigerator, pies will keep 2 days.

CHEF'S NOTE: *The sweet potatoes may be baked up to 2 days in advance of preparing this recipe and stored tightly wrapped in the refrigerator until use.*

GLUTEN-FREE

In this delectable dessert with a true Italian flair, the tart balsamic vinegar combined with sweet maple syrup and fresh mint enhances the flavor of fresh, juicy strawberries. Topped with a light vegan whipped "cream," this dish is pleasingly light and refreshing.

BALSAMIC Strawberry Delight with Fresh Mint and Cashew Cream

MAKES 4 TO 6 SERVINGS

CASHEW-VANILLA CREAM

½ cup chopped raw cashews

½ cup water

2 tablespoons maple syrup

½ teaspoon vanilla extract

STRAWBERRIES

2 cups (1 pint) strawberries, halved

2 tablespoons maple syrup

1 tablespoon balsamic vinegar

1 tablespoon chopped fresh mint, plus several sprigs for garnish

Put the cashews and ¼ cup water into a small bowl. Refrigerate for 1 to 4 hours. Drain the cashews and rinse thoroughly in cold water. Put the soaked and drained cashews, maple syrup, ¼ cup water and vanilla in a blender container. Blend for 30 seconds, or until completely smooth (see note). Cover and refrigerate for 2 hours, or until chilled.

Put the strawberries, 2 tablespoons maple syrup, vinegar and chopped mint into a medium-sized bowl and gently stir to combine. Cover and refrigerate for about 1 hour to allow the flavors to marry (see note).

When ready to serve, spoon strawberries into 4 to 6 petite glasses or dessert dishes. Drizzle the cashew cream over the top, garnish with a mint sprig and serve!

CHEF'S NOTE: *For a thick, whipped-topping consistency, blend the cashews with 2 tablespoons water (in place of the ¼ cup). Start to blend and add more water, if needed. For a thinner topping consistency, add an additional tablespoon (or 2) of water before blending.*

CHEF'S NOTE: *If desired, you can serve the strawberries right away; however, the flavors will be less developed.*

GLUTEN-FREE

No baking required for these squishy, sweet and crunchy cereal bites. So easy to make, plus they are healthy *and* delicious!

DATE 'N RICE Cereal Treats

MAKES 12 TO 16 TREATS

¼ cup maple syrup

¼ cup plus 1 tablespoon creamy peanut butter

½ teaspoon vanilla extract

⅔ cup pitted and finely chopped Medjool dates

2 cups crisp brown rice cereal (use gluten-free cereal if you are gluten-free)

CHEF'S NOTE: *These treats are quite soft and somewhat crumbly even after they are chilled.*

Line an 8-inch square baking pan with unbleached parchment paper, leaving an overhang of 2-inch "wings" on two opposite sides of the pan. Put the maple syrup, peanut butter and vanilla into a medium-sized bowl and mix together using a large rubber spatula or spoon. Fold in the dates. Gently fold in the rice cereal.

Spread the cereal mixture in an even layer in the prepared pan and press firmly to make the treats more compact. Cover and refrigerate for at least 4 hours or overnight before dividing into little "bites" (see note). Serve cold. Stored in a tightly covered container and refrigerated, treats will keep for 3 days.

3 INGREDIENTS OR LESS

GLUTEN-FREE

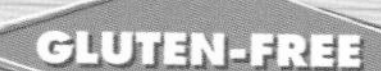

Two tasty ingredients are all it takes to make this frosty and frothy dessert shake!

VANILLA-BANANA *Shake*

MAKES 2 SERVINGS

2 very large (or 3 medium) **ripe bananas, peeled, sliced and frozen**

¾ cup sweetened vanilla-flavored nondairy milk, plus more as needed

Put the frozen banana slices and 1 cup nondairy milk in a high-performance blending appliance. Process until smooth and creamy, adding more nondairy milk as needed to achieve desired consistency. Serve immediately.

VARIATION: *Chocolate-Banana Smoothie Shake: Use sweetened chocolate-flavored nondairy milk in place of the vanilla variety.*

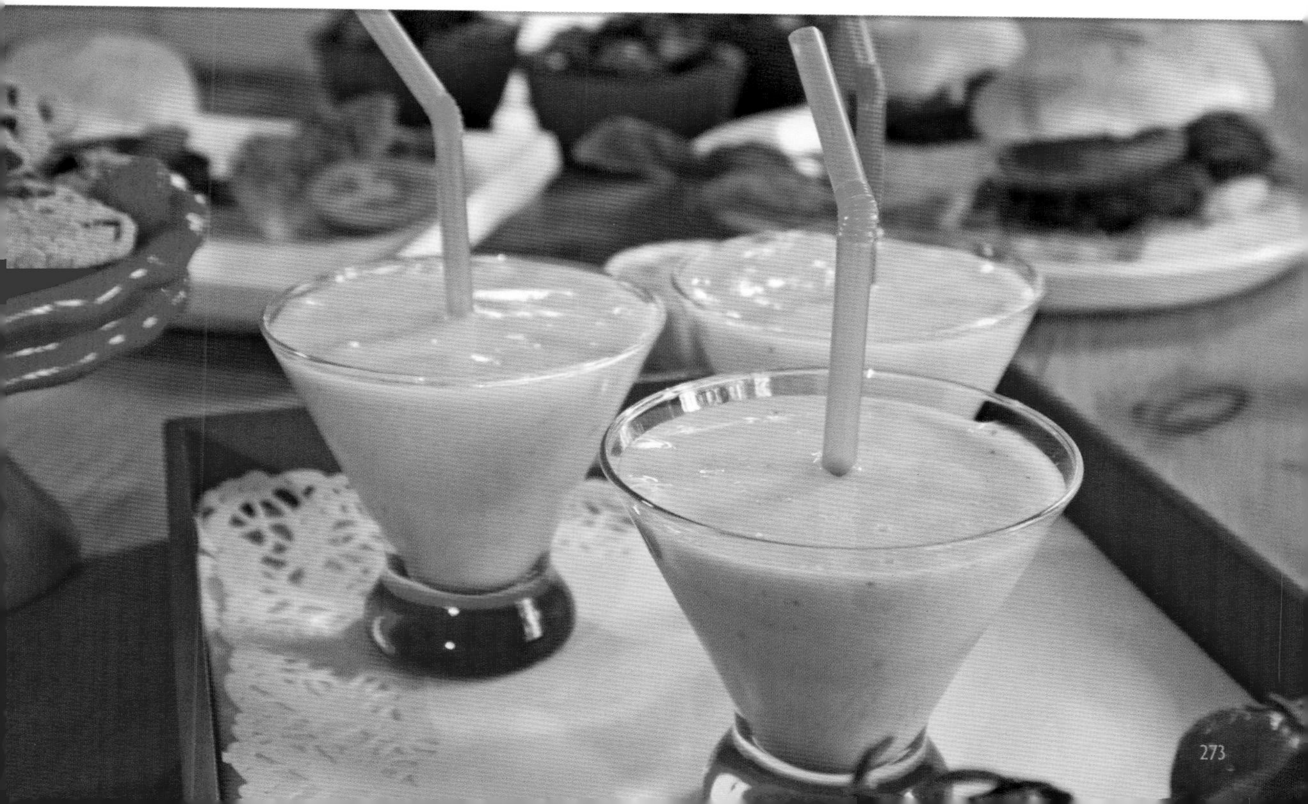

Chocolate, chocolate, chocolate! Everyone loves chocolate. Whether it's a luscious cake, creamy pie, velvety pudding or frozen treat, a chocolaty dessert is my go-to when I want to "wow" my family and friends. In this chapter, I'll share some of my favorite decadent, rich chocolate sweets that are perfect to serve as an extraordinary close to any festive meal!

CHAPTER

SIXTEEN

Ultimate Chocolate DESSERTS

Chocolate Ganache Cake, *page 284*

GLUTEN-FREE

If I had to choose my favorite dessert of all time, this would be the one. A maple-y vegan variation of my original rendition (based on my grandma's chocolaty recipe), this pudding is so creamy, your guests will not believe that it's based in (shhhh) tofu! Bonus: it takes only 10 minutes to prep!

MAPLE-CHOCOLATE Pots de Crème

MAKES 6 TO 10 SERVINGS

- **¾ cup unsweetened nondairy milk**
- **14 ounces firm or extra-firm regular tofu, drained and cubed** (see note)
- **2 tablespoons maple syrup**
- **1 teaspoon vanilla extract**
- **1 cup vegan chocolate chips** (55% to 65% cacao)
- **Fresh raspberries, for garnish** (optional)
- **Mint sprigs, for garnish** (optional)

Put the nondairy milk in a small saucepan and bring to a simmer over medium-low heat. Put the tofu, maple syrup and vanilla extract in a blender, and then add the chocolate chips. Pour in the simmering nondairy milk and process for 45 seconds to 1 minute, or until *completely* smooth.

Spoon or pour the mixture into eight to ten mini dessert glasses or espresso cups—or six to eight small dessert bowls—and garnish with a raspberry and mint sprig, or a single chocolate chip. Refrigerate for 4 to 6 hours. Serve cold.

CHEF'S NOTE: *If you are cooking gluten free, make certain to purchase certified gluten-free tofu, available in most supermarkets.*

GLUTEN-FREE

These delightful chocolaty, velvety and creamy cakes are tiny in size, but bold in flavor! They make an inviting afternoon snack, weeknight dessert *or* fancy finish to an elegant dinner party.

No-Bake CINNAMON-CHOCOLATE PUDDING CAKES

MAKES 12 MINI-CAKES

CRUST

½ cup chopped walnuts

½ cup unsweetened shredded dried coconut

8 Medjool dates, pitted and chopped

1 tablespoon maple syrup

CHEF'S NOTE: *If you are cooking gluten free, make certain to purchase certified gluten-free tofu, available in most supermarkets.*

Put all of the crust ingredients in a high-performance blending appliance and process to the consistency of cookie dough, stopping the machine and scraping the bowl several times. The dough will be very sticky. Transfer to a small bowl. Evenly divide and press the dough into a 12-cup, nonstick mini-cheesecake pan that has twelve removable bottoms (see note) to make a crust.

CHEFS NOTE: *If you do not have a mini cheesecake pan with removable bottoms, you can use a 12-cup mini muffin tin. Line each of the cups with two criss-crossed strips of unbleached parchment paper, leaving a 1-inch overhang of the strips, making paper "wings." When the pudding cakes are completely chilled, lift each cake out of the cups, using the paper "wings." Carefully remove the paper and serve.*

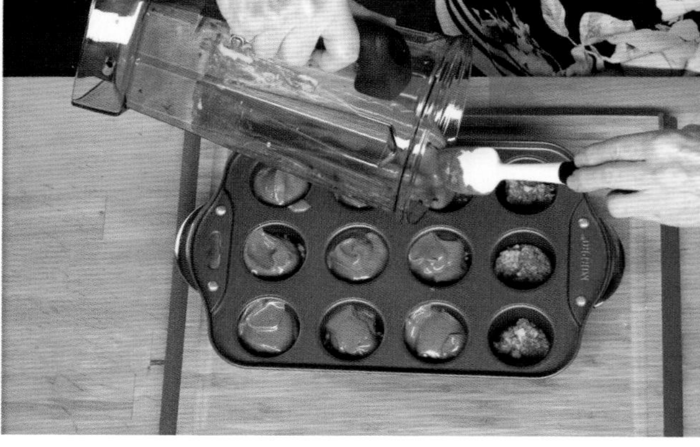

PUDDING

¼ cup sweetened vanilla-flavored nondairy milk

⅓ block (about 6 ounces) **regular extra-firm tofu, drained well and crumbled** (see note)

1 tablespoon vegan cane sugar

½ teaspoon vanilla extract

¼ teaspoon ground cinnamon

Dash cayenne pepper (optional)

½ cup vegan chocolate chips (55% to 65% cacao)

TOPPING

12 vegan white or dark chocolate chips, for garnish

Put the nondairy milk in a small saucepan and bring to a simmer over medium-low heat. Put the tofu, sugar, vanilla, cinnamon, optional cayenne and chocolate chips *in the order listed* into the blender container. Pour the simmering hot milk over the chocolate chip mixture, and immediately process for about 1 minute, or until the pudding is *very* smooth. Immediately pour one-twelfth of the chocolate pudding mixture over the crust in each of the twelve cheesecake cups. Smooth out the top of each pudding cake and garnish each with a single white or dark chocolate chip. Cover loosely and refrigerate for 6 to 8 hours before carefully removing the cakes. Serve cold. Stored in a tightly covered container in the refrigerator, pudding cakes will keep for 3 days.

GLUTEN-FREE

The title of this recipe says it all. Wow your guests with a pudding that tastes so decadent, they will not believe it's totally soy free, gluten free *and* vegan! Silky smooth, thick, rich and super chocolaty—this is a flawless dessert that will impress the chocolate fans in your life.

DEEP DARK *Chocolate Truffle* PUDDING

MAKES 6 TO 8 SERVINGS

- 1 cup raw cashews
- 1¾ cups water, divided
- 3 tablespoons vegan brown sugar or cane sugar
- 1 tablespoon unsweetened cocoa powder
- 1 teaspoon vanilla extract
- 4 Medjool dates, pitted and chopped
- 1 cup vegan dark chocolate chips, plus more for garnish

Put the cashews and ¾ cup water in a small bowl. Refrigerate and let soak for 1 to 4 hours. Drain the cashews and rinse thoroughly in cold water.

Put the remaining 1 cup water in a small saucepan and bring to a simmer over medium-low heat. Put the soaked cashews, sugar, cocoa powder, vanilla extract, dates and chocolate chips in a high-performance blender container *in the order listed*. Pour in the simmering water and process for 30 seconds to 1 minute, or until completely smooth. Divide the mixture between six small wine glasses or eight espresso cups. Refrigerate 4 to 8 hours or until set. Serve chilled with *Cashew-Vanilla Cream* (page 271) spooned on top, garnished with more chocolate chips or some cocoa nibs, if desired.

Photos courtesy of Annie Olivero. Learn more about Annie on page 296.

GLUTEN-FREE

This pie is gorgeous to look at, delicious to eat and a delight to serve! Your family and guests will think you slaved for hours creating the "fancy" marbled effect, but it's actually super easy to do! You will please chocolate *and* coffee lovers alike with this impressive sweet indulgence!

Mad Mocha MARBLED MOUSSE PIE

MAKES 10 SERVINGS

CRUST

1 tablespoon extra-virgin olive oil, plus more to coat pan

11 Medjool dates, pitted and chopped

⅔ cup chopped pecans

½ cup chopped walnuts

½ cup unsweetened shredded dried coconut

FILLING

1 block (14 to 15 ounces) **extra-firm regular tofu, drained and crumbled**

5½ tablespoons vegan cane sugar

½ cup cold, strong brewed coffee

1½ cups vegan dark chocolate chips (55% to 70% cacao)

½ cup unsweetened *or* sweetened nondairy milk

CHEF'S NOTE: *If desired, create a decorative edge to the crust. Using the tines of a fork, press gently down around the entire outer edge of the crust to form evenly spaced lines.*

Generously coat a 9-inch round pie pan with olive oil. Put all of the crust ingredients in a high-performance blending appliance and process into a dough, stopping the machine and scraping the bowl several times. The dough will be very sticky. Transfer the dough to the oiled pan and press it into the bottom and up the sides of the pan (see note). Put the pie pan in the freezer for 6 to 8 minutes, and then transfer to the refrigerator while you prepare the filling.

To make the filling, put the tofu, sugar and coffee into a blender and process until very smooth. Transfer ⅓ cup of the tofu/coffee mixture to a small bowl and reserve. Add the chocolate chips to the top of the remaining tofu mixture (that is still *in* the blender container).

Put the nondairy milk into a small saucepan and bring it to a simmer over medium-low heat. Immediately pour the simmering nondairy milk over the chocolate chip mixture and process for 30 seconds to 1 minute, or until it becomes *completely* smooth. Pour the chocolate filling into the chilled crust (it will mound up slightly, *above* the crust). Immediately drop 5 to 6 spoonfuls of the reserved tofu/coffee mixture onto the top of the pie. Then, using a wooden skewer or the tip of a knife, gently *swirl* the tofu/coffee mixture into the top of the pie in a pleasing, marbleized pattern. Refrigerate for at least 3 hours (or overnight), until completely set. Slice and serve!

CHEF'S NOTE: *If you are cooking gluten free, make certain to purchase certified gluten-free tofu, available in most supermarkets.*

This rich, decadent and gorgeous cake is a truly scrumptious confection, topped with luscious vegan chocolate ganache frosting. This outstanding cake is ideal to serve as an enticing dessert at any gathering throughout the year.

CHOCOLATE *Ganache* CAKE

MAKES 8 TO 10 SERVINGS

CAKE

1 teaspoon vegan buttery spread, for coating pan

2 cups whole wheat pastry flour

⅔ cup unsweetened cocoa powder

1 teaspoon baking powder

1 teaspoon baking soda

½ teaspoon sea salt

1¼ cups vegan brown sugar or cane sugar

1½ cups sweetened chocolate- or vanilla-flavored nondairy milk, divided, plus more as needed

¼ cup vegan cream cheese, at room temperature

¼ cup extra-virgin olive oil

1 teaspoon vanilla extract

GANACHE

½ cup sweetened vanilla-flavored nondairy milk

1 bar (3.5 ounces) **vegan dark chocolate** (snack-style bar, not unsweetened baking chocolate)

1 tablespoon vegan brown sugar or cane sugar

1 teaspoon extra-virgin olive oil

Preheat the oven to 400 degrees F. Generously coat a 9-inch round baking pan with vegan buttery spread. Put the flour, cocoa powder, baking powder, baking soda and salt in a large bowl and stir with a dry whisk to combine. Add the sugar and whisk to combine. Put ¼ cup of the nondairy milk, vegan cream cheese, olive oil and vanilla in a blender and process until smooth. Add to the flour mixture, along with an additional 1¼ cups of nondairy milk. Stir until well combined and somewhat fluffy. The mixture will be a bit stiff, but if it seems overly dry, stir in additional nondairy milk, 1 tablespoon at a time, up to 3 tablespoons. Pour the mixture into the prepared pan and smooth the top. Bake for 15 minutes. Decrease the heat to 350 degrees F and bake for an additional 25 minutes or until a toothpick inserted in the center of the cake comes out clean. (If it seems that the cake is starting to *burn* during the last 10 minutes of baking, tent it with foil.) Put the pan on a wire rack. Allow the cake to cool completely.

After the cake cools, prepare the ganache. Heat ½ cup nondairy milk in a small saucepan over medium-low heat until simmering. Chop the vegan chocolate bar into small pieces. Put the chocolate pieces, 1 tablespoon sugar and 1 teaspoon olive oil in a large bowl. Slowly pour in the simmering nondairy milk, whisking vigorously after each addition, until the chocolate is smooth and shiny. Immediately drizzle or spread the frosting over the cake. Refrigerate for 1 hour or until set. Covered tightly and stored in the refrigerator, leftover cake will keep for about 2 days.

My grandma made a German chocolate cake that was simply out of this world. I adored it, so I created a vegan version that tastes much like the original.

German Chocolate CAKE

MAKES 10 SERVINGS

FROSTING

⅓ cup vegan buttery spread, plus more to coat pan

½ cup (about 4 ounces) crumbled soft regular tofu, drained

¼ cup maple syrup

1 teaspoon vanilla extract

1 cup unsweetened shredded dried coconut

¾ cup finely chopped or diced pecans

3 tablespoons vegan brown sugar, cane sugar or maple sugar

CAKE

1 cup whole wheat flour

1 cup unbleached pastry flour

1 teaspoon baking powder

1 teaspoon baking soda

¼ teaspoon sea salt

¾ cup vegan brown sugar, cane sugar or maple sugar

½ cup unsweetened cocoa powder

¼ cup unsweetened shredded dried coconut

1¼ cups sweetened plain nondairy milk

2 tablespoons extra-virgin olive oil

1 tablespoon freshly squeezed lemon juice

10 pecan halves, for garnish

¼ cup vegan chocolate curls, for garnish (see note)

1 to 2 tablespoons flaked dried coconut, for garnish (optional)

To make the frosting, put the vegan buttery spread, tofu, maple syrup and vanilla extract in a blender and process until smooth. Transfer to a medium-sized bowl. Add the coconut, pecans and sugar and stir until combined. Cover and refrigerate for 3 to 4 hours to set up.

Preheat the oven to 375 degrees F. Generously coat a 9-inch round cake pan with vegan buttery spread. Put the flours, baking powder, baking soda and salt in a large bowl and stir with a dry whisk to combine. Add the sugar, cocoa powder and coconut and whisk to combine. Stir in the nondairy milk, olive oil and lemon juice and mix just until incorporated. Don't overmix or the cake will be tough.

Pour the batter into the prepared pan. Bake for 30 to 35 minutes or until a toothpick inserted in the middle of the cake comes out clean. Put the pan on a wire rack and loosen the sides of the cake with a knife. Cool for 15 minutes. Carefully remove the cake from the pan and put it on the wire rack. Let cool *completely* before frosting.

Spoon the cold frosting over the top of the cake. Gently spread the frosting in an even layer, using an offset spatula (the frosting will be *very* thick). Garnish with pecan halves, chocolate curls and optional flaked coconut. Serve immediately, or cover and refrigerate for 1 to 3 hours and serve cold. Covered tightly and stored in the refrigerator, the cake will keep for 2 days.

CHEF'S NOTE: *To make chocolate curls, slice a vegan chocolate snack bar into small "curls" using a carrot peeler.*

Oh wow—these cupcakes are amazing! That's what I said the first time I made these simple but super tempting treats. Avocado and vegan "buttermilk" stand in effortlessly for the butter and egg, while tofu and dark chocolate chips whip up to provide a semi-sweet, rich and decadent tasting frosting—a real crowd pleaser!

CHOCOLATE-AVOCADO *Cupcakes* WITH FLUFFY FROSTING

MAKES 6 SERVINGS

FROSTING

⅓ cup sweetened chocolate- or vanilla-flavored nondairy milk

⅔ block (about 10 ounces) **extra-firm regular tofu**

2 tablespoons vegan confectioner's (powdered) **sugar**

½ cup vegan chocolate chips (55% to 60% cacao)

CUPCAKES

½ cup sweetened chocolate- or vanilla-flavored nondairy milk

2 teaspoons freshly squeezed lemon juice

½ rounded cup peeled, pitted and chopped avocado (½-inch chunks)

1 cup water, divided

1 cup plus 3 tablespoons whole wheat flour, plus more as needed

⅔ cup vegan cane sugar

¼ cup plus 1½ tablespoons unsweetened cocoa powder

½ teaspoon baking powder

1 teaspoon vanilla extract

To make the frosting, heat ⅓ cup of nondairy milk in a small saucepan over medium-low heat until simmering. Put the tofu, powdered sugar and chocolate chips in a blender *in the order listed.* Pour in the simmering nondairy milk and process until *very* smooth. Put a piping bag that has been fitted with a star tip into a tall glass, so it remains upright. Spoon the frosting into the piping bag (see note). Refrigerate the frosting for 2 to 3 hours, or until it is thoroughly cold and firm enough to pipe onto the cupcakes.

To make the cupcakes, preheat the oven to 375 degrees F. Line a 6-cup standard muffin tin with paper liners. Put ½ cup nondairy milk and the lemon juice into a small bowl and stir to combine. Let the mixture stand for 5 to 10 minutes to make a light vegan "buttermilk."

Put the avocado and ½ cup water in a blender and process until smooth and creamy in texture. Put the flour, sugar, cocoa powder and baking powder in a large bowl and stir with a dry whisk to combine. Make a well in the center of the bowl. Stir in the avocado mixture, the "buttermilk" mixture, ½ cup water and vanilla extract. If the batter is a bit loose, stir in a bit more flour, 1 tablespoon at a time, until the batter thickens up. Divide the mixture equally into the lined cups. Bake for 35 to 37 minutes or until a toothpick inserted in the middle of a cupcake comes out clean. Transfer to a wire rack and let cool 10 minutes, and then remove the cupcakes and put them on a wire rack. Cool *completely.*

Once the cupcakes have cooled, pipe one-sixth of the frosting over each cupcake. Serve immediately, or

tightly cover and refrigerate until serving. (For best taste, remove the cupcakes from the refrigerator about 15 minutes before serving.) Stored tightly covered in the refrigerator, cupcakes will keep for 2 to 3 days.

CHEF'S NOTE: *To save time, put the frosting in a small bowl. Refrigerate 2 to 3 hours. Spoon some frosting over each cupcake and spread with an offset spatula.*

A fantastic dessert or after-school snack, these yummy vegan brownies will delight kiddos and adults alike! With a pop of chocolaty-peanut butter frosting, spread over moist, cake-like brownie squares, this sweet treat is a real winner.

COCOA-CAKE *Brownie Bites* with Chocolate-Peanut Butter Frosting

MAKES 24 TO 32 BROWNIE BITES

BROWNIES

1 teaspoon *cold* vegan buttery spread, for coating pan

1¼ cups whole wheat pastry flour *or* regular whole wheat flour (see note)

¼ cup plus 2 tablespoons unsweetened cocoa powder

1 teaspoon baking powder

¼ teaspoon baking soda

⅛ teaspoon sea salt

2 tablespoons flaxseeds

⅔ cup firmly packed vegan dark brown sugar

¾ cup sweetened plain nondairy milk, plus more as needed

½ cup *melted* vegan buttery spread

½ cup chopped pecans

FROSTING

½ cup vegan chocolate chips (55% to 70% cacao)

2 tablespoons plus 1 teaspoon creamy peanut butter (see note)

3 tablespoons sweetened plain nondairy milk

1 tablespoon maple syrup

Preheat the oven to 350 degrees F. Coat a 9-inch square baking pan with vegan buttery spread. Line the pan with unbleached parchment paper, leaving 2-inch wings on two sides of the pan.

Put the flour, cocoa powder, baking powder, baking soda and salt in a large bowl and stir with a dry whisk to combine. Put the flaxseeds in a high-performance blending appliance and process into fine flour. Add the ground flaxseeds to the flour/cocoa mixture and stir with the whisk to combine. Add the sugar and whisk until almost no lumps remain. Add the nondairy milk and melted buttery spread and stir with a large spoon, just until moistened and no bits of dry flour remain. (Add 1 to 2 tablespoons more of the nondairy milk, if the mixture seems dry.) Fold in the pecans.

CHEF'S NOTE: *You may use regular whole wheat flour in place of the pastry flour. The brownies are slightly more dense, but delicious!*

Pour the batter into the prepared pan and smooth the top with a rubber spatula. Bake for 17 to 20 minutes or until a toothpick inserted into the center of the brownies comes out clean. Put the pan on a wire rack. Let cool for 8 to 10 minutes.

Meanwhile, to make the frosting, put the chocolate chips, peanut butter, nondairy milk and maple syrup into a double boiler. Cook over low heat until the chocolate chips melt, stirring occasionally to thoroughly combine

CHEF'S NOTE: *You may use your preferred nut or seed butter in place of the peanut butter, if desired.*

the frosting. Let cool 3 to 5 minutes. Spread the frosting over the brownies while they are still warm in the pan. Put the brownies in the freezer for 5 to 10 minutes to allow the frosting to begin to set.

Set the brownie pan back on the wire rack. Holding on to the paper "wings," lift up and transfer the brownies to a cutting board. Cut the brownies into 26 to 32 small rectangles, using a sharp serrated knife. Transfer the brownies to a platter, cover and refrigerate for at least 30 minutes before serving. Covered and stored in the refrigerator, the brownie bites will keep for about 3 days.

GLUTEN-FREE

These refreshing mini treats are sure to dazzle your family and guests alike. A crisp chocolate cookie juxtaposed with a cold and creamy "ice cream" filling makes these frozen confections the darling of any party. Plus, they are a breeze to prepare!

Little Vegan "ICE CREAM" SANDWICHES

MAKES 6 TO 8 SERVINGS

12 to 16 vegan crème filled chocolate (sandwich-style) **cookies** (see note)

12 to 16 heaping tablespoons slightly softened, nondairy vanilla or chocolate "ice-cream" (or your favorite flavor, see note)

Line a medium-sized, rimmed baking sheet with unbleached parchment paper. Gently twist open the crème filled chocolate cookies. Spoon a small scoop of "ice cream" onto each cookie and reattach the cookie tops. Arrange in a single layer on the lined baking sheet. Freeze for 1 hour, or until firm. Remove the cookies from the freezer and arrange on a pretty platter. Alternately, put 2 sandwiches on each of six to eight dessert plates and serve (see note).

CHEF'S NOTE: *For a gluten-free option, use both certified gluten-free cookies and nondairy, gluten-free "ice-cream" in this recipe.*

CHEF'S NOTE: *Once the sandwiches are removed from the freezer, let them stand at room temperature for 2 to 3 minutes to soften up a bit before serving.*

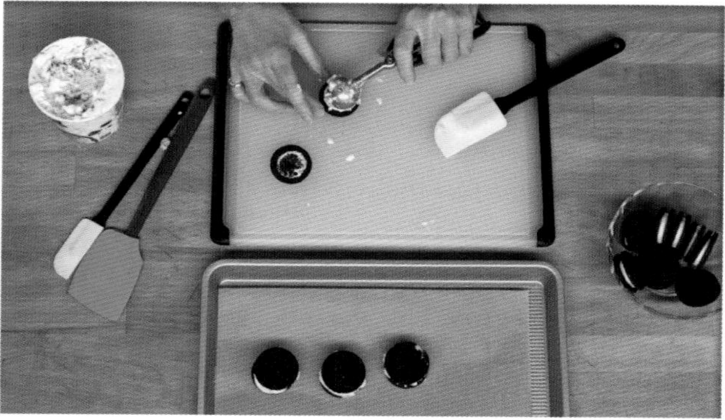

GLUTEN-FREE

This holiday inspired homemade chocolate "candy" makes a delicious treat any time of year and will inspire the kiddos to be creative in the kitchen! Create a personalized adaptation of the recipe by using your preferred nuts, seeds or dried fruits. I have included my version here, but feel free to change up these easy-to-prepare snacks to please your family.

CHOCOLATE *Polka Dot* BARK

MAKES 12 SERVINGS

BASIC BARK RECIPE

1 cup vegan chocolate chips (55% to 70% cacao)

35 to 45 vegan white chocolate chips (the white chips make the polka dots)

¼ cup sweetened dried cranberries *or* raisins

3 tablespoons chopped pecans *or* roasted (or raw) **cashews**

Line two 9-inch square baking pans with unbleached parchment paper, leaving an overhang of 1-inch "wings" on two sides of the pans, and secure the wings to the pan with metal clips. Melt the chocolate in a double boiler over low heat, stirring often. Pour the melted chocolate onto the prepared baking pans and immediately, gently tip the pan(s) to spread the chocolate in a thin, even layer over the parchment, leaving about a ½-inch between the edge of the chocolate and the side of the pan.

Arrange the white chocolate chips in a polka dot pattern over the top, gently pressing them into the warm chocolate. Put the cranberries or raisins in between the white chocolate chips, and then sprinkle with the pecans or cashews, pressing gently into the chocolate. Freeze for 15 to 20 minutes (or refrigerate for 1 hour) until set, and then gently peel off the parchment from the bottom of the chocolate. Put the chocolate on a plate and randomly break it into pieces of "bark." Serve immediately, or refrigerate the bark in a tightly closed container (between sheets of parchment paper) for up to 1 week.

Julie
Rob
Mark
Laura
Mom

Acknowledments

My deepest gratitude goes out to friends, family and colleagues for their continued support of my vegan journey! An eternal thank you goes to my husband Andy, whose faith in me makes all of my hard work come to life.

To my family and friends, I hope you know how much your unconditional love and encouragement has meant to me all these years. You are my community and my rock. Thank you to my beautiful, incredible sister Julie and awesome brother-in-law Rob for your hard work and support for my vegan commitment and creative endeavors. A special thank you to my mother for her constant faith in me and for sharing her wonderful recipe ideas that have spanned over many years! Deep appreciation goes to my mother-in-law Anita and father-in-law Jack for always believing in me, supporting me and inspiring me to continue on this uncertain journey. Thank you so much to my late father, Bill, and step-mom, Chris, whose enthusiasm for my creative life-path never waivered.

A big thank you goes to the wonderful Scribe Publishing Company team—for your talent and guidance throughout the process of writing this book. Ultimate appreciation goes to Jennifer Baum, whose outstanding talents, organizational skills, editing prowess and creative vision brought this book to full fruition. Thank you to John Wincek for his brilliant design and to Mel Corrigan for her talent, dedication, editing and proofreading with such patience and caring. And I am grateful for our additional proofreaders: Grace Edinger, Judy Filipski-Baum, Allison Janicki, Chris Lacy and William Lacy.

Thank you so much to Regina Eisenberg, who was and still is instrumental in making this show happen with her continued commitment to *Jazzy Vegetarian,* helping to bring the television series from dream to reality. I gratefully appreciate Gayle Loeber, Bob Petts and the entire NETA team for their excellent job in distributing the *Jazzy Vegetarian* television program on public television, Create TV, PBS and beyond.

Left: Laura's mother and sister help to set the table for a family holiday gathering.

Gratitude goes out to our Season Eight underwriters, *Earth Fare* and *Papa Vince Foods,* for supporting us to make this season happen! And thank you to Soom Foods for helping to sponsor Season Seven. A big jazzy thank you also goes to the fabulous Kelly Barron, our underwriter producer this season.

Many thanks to our wonderful brand partners for Season Seven *and* Season Eight: Melissa's Produce, April Cornell, Carpe Diem Hardware, Anolon, Oxo, Vitamix, BK Resources, Pascha Chocolate, Cardinal International, Wholesome, Simply Organic, Graftobian, Nucu, Vollrath, Beverage Air, Time Worn Tables, Kitchen All, Quick n' Crispy, Swiss Diamond Cookware and Miso Master.

A heart-filled thanks to my growing network of amazing vegan authors, recipe developers and bloggers—Dianne Wenz, Nava Atlas, Annie Oliverio, Zel Allen, Zsu Dever and so many more—for your hard work in promoting veganism and for continued support through the years.

As always, thank you to the animals. I do this all for you, in hopes of doing my part to help create a more compassionate world for everyone.

ABOUT THE CONTRIBUTORS

It is with tremendous gratitude that I thank the incredibly brilliant Julieanna Hever for contributing the excellent "Plant-Based Nutrition 101" section for this book. **Julieanna Hever MS, RD, CPT,** The Plant-Based Dietitian, has a BA in Theatre and MS in Nutrition, bridging her biggest passions for food, presenting and helping people. She has authored five books, including the brand new *Healthspan Solution, Plant-Based Nutrition (Idiot's Guide)* and *The Vegiterranean Diet,* plus two peer-reviewed journal articles on plant-based nutrition for healthcare professionals. She was the host of *What Would Julieanna Do?,* gave a TEDx talk and instructed for the eCornell Plant-Based Nutrition Certification Program. She's appeared on *The Dr. Oz Show, Harry (Connick) Show* and *The Steve Harvey Show.* Julieanna is the Co-Founder and Nutrition Director for Efferos, and she speaks and consults with clients around the globe.

A special thank goes to the fabulously talented **Annie Oliverio,** who graciously contributed eight beautiful photos to this book. Annie Oliverio is the author of *Crave Eat Heal: Plant-based, Whole Food Recipes to Satisfy Every Appetite* and founder of the website *An Unrefined Vegan.* Learn more about Annie, her recipes, books and her photography at anunrefinedvegan.com.

Right: Laura with *Chocolate-Avocado Cupcakes* (page 288).

NUTRITION AND THE PLANT-BASED DIET

One of the most commonly asked questions regarding a vegan diet is where to get your nutrients like protein, B12, vitamin D, iron, selenium, iodine, omega-3 fats or calcium. I believe that this is best answered by a registered dietitian, so I am honored that Julieanna Hever, M.S., R.D., C.P.T., will share some words of wisdom with us here. For more comprehensive information about the nutritional benefits of a plant-based diet, Julieanna's book, *The Healthspan Solution,* makes excellent supplemental reading to *Vegan For Everyone.*

PLANT-BASED NUTRITION 101

by Julieanna Hever, MS, RD, CPT

A "well-planned" plant-based diet consists of vegetables, fruits, whole grains, legumes, mushrooms, nuts, seeds, herbs and spices.[1] Half of your plate (or diet) should consist of vegetables and fruits, which is in agreement with the Unites States Department of Agriculture, American Cancer Society and American Heart Association. Veggies (especially leafy greens and cruciferous varieties) and fruits are the most nutrient-dense foods on the planet. They are chock-full of phytonutrients, fiber, potassium, magnesium, iron, folate and vitamins C and A. The *Plant-Based Food Plate* (opposite page) provides general parameters for what a typical day-in-the-life should ideally look like.

What about Protein?

Recommended protein intake[2] is based on your weight. Although it is quite popular for people to pursue protein in hefty doses, we only need approximately 10 percent of kcals to come from protein in order to meet our needs. (In fact, excessive protein can be harmful, taxing the kidneys, promoting gout and other chronic diseases, particularly when sourced

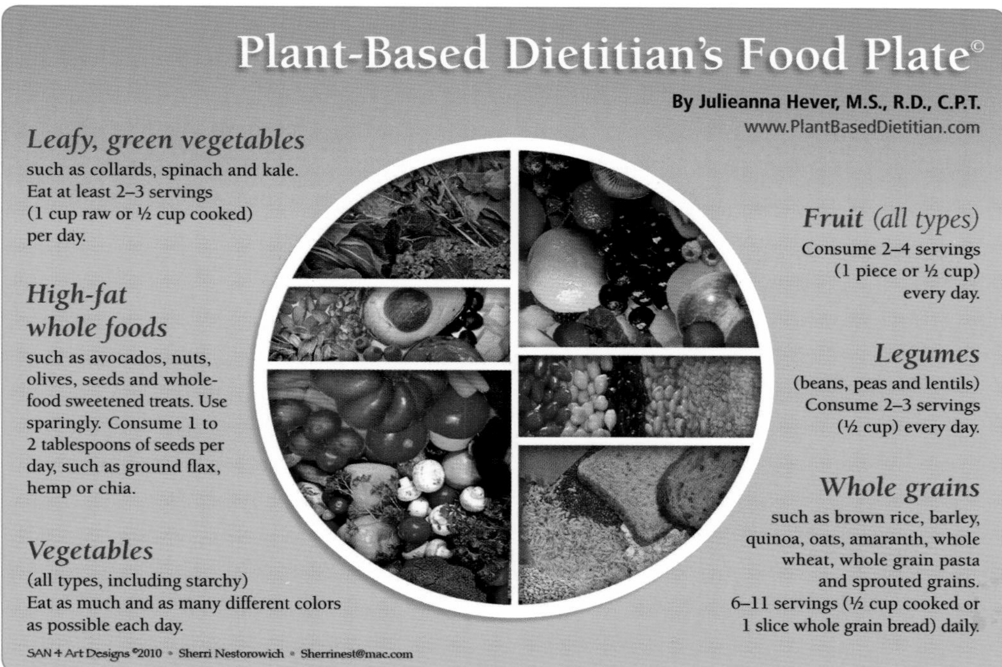

from animal products). Protein is found abundantly throughout the plant world. Foods that are protein powerhouses include legumes, nuts and nut butters, seeds and seed butters, soy foods and intact whole grains.

How Do I Get Vitamin B12?

Cobalamin, the technical name for vitamin B12, is the only nutrient not directly available from plants. Basically, if you don't eat animal products, are over the age of 50 (regardless of your diet) and are not supplementing, you are at a high risk for deficiency. Fortunately, however, this is easily remedied. With a vegan diet, vitamin B12 can be found in fortified plant milks, cereals or nutritional yeast. Still, these may not be dependable sources of B12. The most reliable, cost-effective, easiest and safest method of avoiding deficiency for vegans is to take a B12 supplement. To optimize absorption, I recommend taking either 50 micrograms twice a day, 150 micrograms once a day or 2,000 to 2,500 micrograms once per week. Vitamin B12 is water soluble, so toxicity is rare.

Where Do I Get My Vitamin D?

Vitamin D, scientifically known as calciferol, is also considered the "sunshine vitamin." This is because it is the only nutrient that is obtained from exposure to the sun. Although vitamin D is treated as a vitamin, it is technically a prohormone because it is produced by your skin as the result of exposure to ultraviolet B (UVB) sun radiation and then converted into its active form by your liver and kidneys. Ask your physician to check your blood levels of vitamin D at your next visit. If you turn out to be low, try sun therapy first: Find a way to be outside in the sunshine in the middle of peak hours (usually between 10 a.m. and 3 p.m.) for five to thirty minutes, at least twice per week. Do this with as much sunscreen-free skin exposed as possible, though keep your face and eyes protected with sunscreen, sunglasses and/or a hat. Make sure your skin does not turn pink. Err on the side of less time to avoid sunburn until you find what is best for you. If sun therapy is not effective at bringing up your blood D levels, you may consider supplementing. Ask your physician or dietitian for a recommended dose; because vitamin D is fat soluble, excess amounts are stored in fatty tissue. As a result, you do not want to take more than you need.

How Can I Get Enough Calcium?

Calcium is the most abundant mineral found in the human body. Calcium is one of many nutrients of concern with respect to bone health. Excellent plant sources of calcium include leafy green vegetables—especially bok choy, broccoli, napa cabbage, collard greens, dandelion greens, kale, turnip greens and watercress—as well as fortified plant milks, calcium-set tofu, dried figs, sesame seeds and tahini, tempeh, almonds and almond butter, oranges, sweet potatoes and beans. Regardless of how much calcium you consume, what matters most is how much you actually absorb. There are certain key factors that impact calcium absorption, including:

- How much you consume. You can only absorb about 500 milligrams at a time and absorption decreases as calcium intake increases.
- Your age. Calcium absorption peaks in infants and children, as they are rapidly growing bone, and then progressively decreases as we age.
- Phytates, compounds found in whole grains, beans, seeds, nuts and wheat bran, can bind with calcium as well as with other minerals and inhibit absorption. Soaking, sprouting, leavening and fermenting improve absorption.
- Oxalates are elements found in some leafy green vegetables (such as spinach, Swiss chard, collard greens, parsley, leeks and beet greens), berries, almonds, cashews, peanuts, soybeans, okra, quinoa, cocoa, tea and chocolate. They may also somewhat inhibit absorption of calcium and other minerals, though some may still be absorbed. Aim for variety in the foods you eat on a day-to-day basis to improve overall absorption.

- Monitor your blood levels of vitamin D, which must be optimal to absorb calcium.
- Be careful of excessive intakes of sodium, protein, caffeine and phosphorus (as from sodas) because these nutrients may enhance calcium loss as well.

Fats

There are two groups of essential fatty acids, meaning they are required in the diet because your body cannot produce them. They are categorized in the polyunsaturated chemical group, and are more specifically classified as omega-3 and omega-6 fatty acids.

Omega-3 fats are found in the plant kingdom in the form of alpha linolenic acid (ALA). They can be found in flaxseeds, hempseeds, chia seeds, leafy green vegetables (both land and sea), soybeans and soy foods, walnuts and wheat germ, as well as in their respective oils. It is also possible to find a direct plant source of EPA and DHA, like fish do, from microalgae. Plant sources are ideal because they do not contain the contaminants that fish contain, including heavy metals, such as mercury, lead and cadmium as well as industrial pollutants like DDT, PCBs, dioxin, and possibly even radioactive nucleotides from previous nuclear spills. Another enormous reason to pick plants over fish is because plant sources are sustainable, unlike fish, of which our oceans are imminently running out.[3]

Iron

Plant-sourced iron comes in the form of non-heme iron. Because this form is more vulnerable to compounds that may inhibit its absorption, vegans and vegetarians should increase their iron intake to 1.8 times the RDA. Fortunately, this is easy to do with the wide array of iron-rich food choices like leafy greens, legumes, soy products, dark chocolate, blackstrap molasses, tahini, pumpkin seeds, sunflower seeds, raisins, prunes and cashews. One of the best ways to improve iron absorption is to eat iron-rich foods at the same time as you eat foods high in vitamin C and organic acids. Some examples of these optimal food combinations include a green smoothie with leafy greens (iron) and fruit (vitamin C), bean chili (iron) with tomato sauce (vitamin C) or salad greens (iron) with tomatoes (vitamin C).

Iodine

Due to varying and unreliable soil quality, dietary sources of the trace mineral iodine fluctuate geographically. Vegans need to be aware of finding a source of iodine to avoid thyroid issues. Plant sources of iodine include *iodized* salt and sea vegetables. (The container of salt must state that it is iodized.) One half teaspoon of iodized salt provides the daily recommended 150-microgram dose. If you do not enjoy eating sea vegetables or you are trying to minimize your intake of salt, an iodine supplement may be a good way to ensure adequate intake.

Selenium

Selenium is a mineral that happens to be a powerful antioxidant that protects against cellular damage. It also helps regulate thyroid hormones and plays a role in reproduction and DNA synthesis. Brazil nuts are an especially rich source of selenium in the plant kingdom. Just one ounce (approximately 6 to 8 nuts) provides 777 percent of the RDA. In fact, all it takes is one Brazil nut a day to meet your selenium recommendations. Other plant sources include whole grains, legumes, vegetables, seeds and other nuts.

Zinc

Zinc is a mineral that supports immune function and wound healing, among many of its other important roles. To avoid deficiency as a vegan, aim for 50 percent more than the RDA of zinc daily by making sure to include legumes, cashews and other nuts, seeds, soy products and whole grains. Methods of preparation of zinc-rich foods, such as soaking, sprouting, leavening and fermenting, can help improve absorption.

In conclusion, aim to follow a well-planned plant-based diet consisting of vegetables, fruits, whole grains, legumes, mushrooms, nuts, seeds, herbs and spices, and be mindful to take a vitamin B12 supplement. To learn more about balancing wholesome plant foods for optimal, sustainable health, go to *plantbaseddietitian.com* and *healthspansolution.com*.

Julieanna Hever, MS, RD, CPT

ENDNOTES

1. Hever J, Cronise RJ. Plant-based nutrition for healthcare professionals: implementing diet as a primary modality in the prevention and treatment of chronic disease. Journal of geriatric cardiology: JGC. 2017 May;14(5):355.

2. Institute of Medicine of the National Academies. "Dietary Reference Intakes: Macronutrients." Accessed on April 15, 2015.

3. Worm B, Barbier EB, Beaumont N, et al. Impacts of Biodiversity Loss on Ocean Ecosystem Services. Science 2006;314(5800): 787-90.

Index

C

Mad Mocha Marbled Mousse Pie, page 283.

About the Author

Laura Theodore is a recognized public television personality, vegan celebrity chef, award-winning cookbook author and nationally renowned jazz singer and actor. She is co-creator of the highly successful *Jazzy Vegetarian* vegan cooking series on national public television. Laura is the author of four previous cookbooks, including *Jazzy Vegetarian's Deliciously Vegan, Laura Theodore's Vegan-Ease, Jazzy Vegetarian Classics* and *Jazzy Vegetarian.*

Laura and *Jazzy Vegetarian* are recipients of the *Taste Award* for *Best Health and Fitness Television Program (Food and Diet),* and the *Jazzy Vegetarian* series was inducted into the *Taste Hall of Fame.* Laura's most recent cookbook, *Jazzy Vegetarian's Deliciously Vegan,* won silver medals at the *2018 IBPA Benjamin Franklin Awards,* the *2018 Midwest Book Awards* and the *2019 Living Now Book Awards.* In addition, Laura was a winner of the *2018 Top 100 Vegetarian Blog Awards.*

Laura has been featured on the cover of three prestigious magazines: *American Vegan, Jazzin'* and *La Fashionista Compassionista.* She has been featured in the *New York Times, New York Daily News, Mother Earth Living, VegNews, Family Circle, Readers Digest* and *PBS Food,* among other highly respected news, food, music and lifestyle-related journals. Laura is featured on *Netflix* in the documentary film *Food Choices,* and she has made guest appearances on ABC, NBC, CBS and FOX, *The Talk* on CBS, *Insider/Entertainment Tonight* and the *WCBS News Radio Health & Wellbeing Report.*

As a globally recognized award-winning jazz singer and songwriter, Laura has recorded six solo CDs, including her award-winning disc, *Tonight's the Night,* which received a *Musician Magazine Award.* Her CD release with the late, great Joe Beck entitled *Golden Earrings* (on the *Whaling City Sound* label) was selected to appear on the 52nd Grammy Award list in the category of "Best Jazz Vocal Album." Laura has toured throughout the country, performing at numerous major events, such as *Night of 100 Stars, Fire and Ice Ball* and *The American Film Awards.*

On the acting side of things, Laura has appeared in over sixty plays and musicals, including Off-Broadway for two years in the hit show *Beehive,* which earned her a coveted *Backstage Bistro Award.* She was honored with the *Denver Critics Drama Circle Award* as "Best Actress in a Musical" for her starring role as Janis Joplin in the world premiere production of *Love, Janis.*

With her love for good food, compassion for animals and enthusiasm for great music, multi-talented author Laura Theodore truly is the *Jazzy Vegetarian.*

Additional Titles

BY LAURA THEODORE

Books

Jazzy Vegetarian's Deliciously Vegan: Plant-Powered Recipes for the Modern, Mindful Kitchen

Laura Theodore's Vegan-Ease: An Easy Guide to Enjoying a Plant-Based Diet

Jazzy Vegetarian Classics: Vegan Twists on American Family Favorites

DVD and CDs

The Best of Jazzy Vegetarian (3-DVD Set)

Golden Earrings (CD, Whaling City Sound)

Tonight's The Night (CD, Bearcat Records)

Live at Vartan Jazz (CD, Vartan Jazz Lable)

What the World Needs Now is Love (CD, Bearcat Records)

To purchase autographed copies of Laura's cookbooks, DVDs or CDs, please visit **www.jazzyvegetarian.com**. Receive updates about appearances, books and more by signing up for Laura's mailing list.

Find Laura Theodore and Jazzy Vegetarian Online

WEBSITES	STREAMING CHANNELS	SOCIAL MEDIA
www.jazzyvegetarian.com	www.jazzyvegetariantv.com	www.twitter.com/Jazzyvegetarian
www.lauratheodore.com	www.youtube.com/thejazzyvegetarian	www.facebook.com/JazzyVegetarian
		www.pinterest.com/JazzyVegetarian